MRI Guide for Technologists

A Step by Step Approach

By

Mootoo S. Chunasamy RT (R) (CT) (MR) MSc.

This book is a work of non-fiction. Names and places have been changed to protect the privacy of all individuals. The events and situations are true.

ISBN: 978-1-4107-8139-0 (e)
ISBN: 978-1-4107-8140-6 (sc)

Library of Congress Control Number: 2003095614

This book is printed on acid free paper.

Print information available on the last page.

1stBooks – rev. 11/07/03

TABLE OF CONTENTS

PREFACE

The field of MRI technology has grown considerably since the advent of the first MRI Scanners in 1983. New software, stronger magnets more advanced coils, the introduction of new pulse sequences and techniques, along with the financial considerations associated with the enormous capital outlay and the labor costs associated with longer procedures makes the MRI technologist an invaluable member of the imaging team. Virtually no other technical imaging specialty requires the level of expertise as the MRI technologist

The few schools that are presently offering courses and certificates in MRI have some strengths and some weaknesses. These schools are strong on classroom work such as physics and theory but weak on practice. This becomes glaringly obvious the day the student arrives at my site for their clinical rotation. Some schools offer no clinical rotation.

I have been involved in the education of MRI technologists for a decade and have been surprised at the minimal level of knowledge demonstrated by many experienced working MRI technologists. For this reason I have written this handbook. I have constructed the book in what I hope is a logical progression.

Although nothing can take the place of total intensive hands-on practice under the supervision of a competent technologist, this handbook should make the daily work smooth, routine and effective.

The introduction starts with the usual perfunctory information that being safety, basic physics, basic anatomy and landmarks, medical terminology and commonly used abbreviations in MRI. I have included glossaries on often-used MRI terms: medical terminology, basic terminology,

The next chapters follow a head to foot approach to scanning the body; instructing the reader on use of coils, land marking, positioning, prescribing and giving tips on scanning methodology throughout the sections.

Mootoo Chunasamy

CHAPTER 1

BASIC PHYSICS

The physics of Magnetic Resonance Imaging is very complex; in fact, Physicists specializing in this area of MRI may spend their entire career on this subject. The American Association of Physicists in Medicine (AAPM) has special certification for Physicists specializing in MRI.

It would therefore be quite presumptuous of me to expect to teach the physics of MRI in one chapter. This chapter is geared to explaining the basic physics of MRI so that you, the technologist, can apply this knowledge when performing an MRI examination. knowledge of basic MRI physics may enable you to recognize routine problems and perhaps troubleshoot them without incurring downtime and delays while waiting for service.

DEFINITIONS

1. Magnet

Definition-An object that is surrounded by a magnetic field and that has the property, either natural or induced, of attracting iron or steel.

In MRI, such materials must always be stable, homogeneous and strongly magnetic. There are certain conditions needed to maintain the magnetic environment.

- Cryogens are used to maintain stability by keeping the magnetic windings cool. Both Helium and Nitrogen have been used however most modern magnets only use Helium. As Helium is a cryogenic material, its temperature is -469° F, -269° C or 4° K.
- Shimming coils are used to maintain homogeneity. There are two types of shimming coils.
  - Active, which is on constantly and is electrical.
  - Passive which are sheets of cores stacked together

- Flux density is large enough to maintain field strength up to 3 Tesla

2. Resonance

Definition- The increase in amplitude of oscillation of an electric or mechanical system exposed to a periodic force whose frequency is equal or very close to the natural undamped (Not tending toward a state of rest) frequency of the system.

In MRI the effect is that a nuclei acted upon by an external force will spin at a frequency equal to its own.

3. Imaging

Definition-The production of images of good diagnostic quality for purposes of interpretation

There are three major requirements for MRI imaging

1. Protons of the human body-Used because they are abundant in the body and possess a magnetic moment of their own.
2. Radio frequency (RF)-RF is always oscillating around the main magnet. Termed B_1 With the application of Radio frequency, protons are stimulated and move from a low to high energy. They now possess a magnitude and direction. RF is electro magnetic radiation, the same used for AM radios and television news stations.
3. Strong magnetic field-This main magnet is termed B_o, which is horizontal in design in most modern magnets. In permanent magnets the magnetic field is vertical.

In order to obtain a signal, the RF must be applied perpendicular to the main magnet, B_0. The speed at which the protons resonate must match the magnetic field strength and the Gyromagnetic ratio. The Gyromagnetic ratio is the ratio of the magnetic moment to the mechanical angular momentum of a system).

The Larmor equation is now applied $P=YB_o$.

$P=Y$ (Y=42.6Mhz constant for a 1.0 Tesla magnet)
B_o=Field strength (e.g. 1.0 T)
If a magnet is 1.5T then it is 63.9 MHz.

FREE INDUCTION DECAY

The very first signal produced is called Free Induction Decay (FID) and is unavoidable. When performing an MRI examination a set of pulse sequences is selected. A pulse sequence is a set of instructions telling the computer how the images should appear.

$$T_2^*$$

T_2*- A form of Free Induction Decay which occurs as result of the following:

1. Dephasing caused by magnetic field in homogeneities
2. FID-Free induction decay caused by the induction (leakage) of eddy current.
3. T_2* is shorter than T_2 time.

PARAMETERS THAT AFFECT CONTRAST

The object of MRI is to apply certain timing parameters that will cause one of the three contrast methods to predominate over the others. There are three basic types.

- T_{1W}

T_1 occurs when longitudinal relaxation recovers. The relaxation time (TR) is the property of a tissue at a given magnetic field strength. The TR controls contrast based on T_1 times of tissues.

1. Low TR Low TE
2. Longitudinal Magnetization
3. Equilibrium
4. 63% re-growth
5. 37% loss
6. Spin Lattice
7. Anatomy
8. Giving up of energy to the surrounding lattice
9. T_1 curve- Notice the curve going longitudinally

- T_{2W}

T_2 weighted imaged occurs when the rate of dephasing predominates over the others. Time to Echo (TE) controls contrast based on T_2 relaxation of tissues.

1. High TR High TE
2. Transverse magnetization
3. 37% gain
4. 63% loss
5. Pathology
6. Exchanging of energy to the surrounding lattice
7. 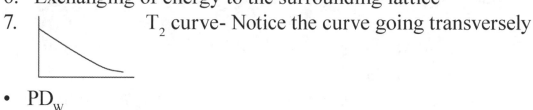 T_2 curve- Notice the curve going transversely

- PD_W

Proton density images occurs when the concentration of nuclei is mainly responsible for the contrast of the image,

1. High TR Low TE
2. Spin spin
3. Intermediate

The RF coils detect and transmit the analogue signal to the host computer. The raw data is stored in the K-space. When the K-space is filled, the examination is finished. There are two types of RF coils. Tranceive and receive only:

- Tranceive coils are larger in design and the signal is uniform throughout but not optimal.
- Receive only coils are smaller in design, they are known as surface coils. They produce optimum signal. They are designed to cover specific region.

K SPACE FILLING

K-Space is the storage of raw data. There are three types of K-space filling. It is filled from the inside out towards the outer of the phased encoding direction. The center of the K Space has the highest contrast but the outer edge has the highest spatial resolution.

1. Sequential-Acquires all the raw data from one slice before going on to the next slice.
2. 2D method-Fills one line of K-space for slice #1 and then moves on to fill slice #2.
3. 3D method-Volumetric acquisition. Acquires data from an entire volume of tissues.

The Fourier transformer performs a mathematical function to convert analogue information into digital information. This information is displayed in rows and columns of pixels. This is the formation of the image.

ARTIFACTS

MRI is very sensitive to motion and other objects that causes degradations on the MR images. These degradations are called artifacts. The following will deal with some causes and solutions.

MOTION ARTIFACTS

Motion artifacts will rob the MR image of quality. It manifests as a smearing or, more commonly, as ghosting. The signal will be mis-mapped along the phase direction. There are two types of motion artifact; voluntary and involuntary.

1. The solution for voluntary motion artifact:

*   Good technologist to patient communication.
*   Saturation pulse technique is employed where a band is placed to cover the moving anatomy near the vicinity of the part being imaged. However saturation effects to the patient is increased and it limits the amount of slices for a given TR.

2. Solutions for involuntary motion artifact are:

*   Saturation pulse technique as described above
*   GATING TECHNIQUE

This means that the echoes are only collected during the resting phase of the cardiac cycle.

*   PULSE TRIGGERING

A transducer is placed on the patient's nail bed or toenail. This technique waits for a pulse wave before it begins to scan. The TR used very limited. The cardiac gate will determine how much TR can be used.

*   ECG TRIGGERING

MRI compatible electrodes are placed on the patient's chest whereby the R wave is detected. Correct placement is important. Usually there are three electrodes that are color-coded and are placed in a triangular manner on the left side of the thorax.

CROSS TALK (ALSO KNOWN AS CROSS EXCITATION)

Energy dissipation to the adjacent slices. For example Lumbar Spine.

Solutions:

- Decrease slice thickness by 30%
- Apply interleave scanning method

(See below)

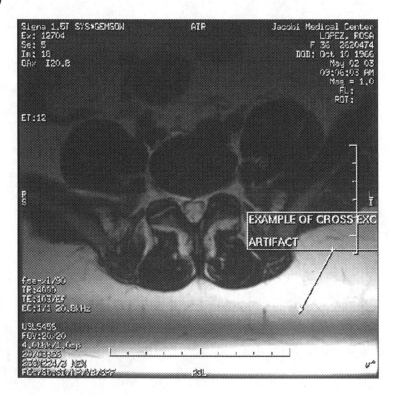

RESPIRATORY GATING

This is controlled by the patient's breathing. The echoes are collected when the patient suspends respiration. This is good for chest, abdomen and spine imaging. This method increases the examination time.

ALIASING OR WRAPAROUND

Aliasing or wrap around is an artifact, which occurs when the patient's anatomy extends out of the FOV within the plane of the image. It is also known as "Fold Over" (See figure 19.9).

Solution:

Increase the field of view or apply saturation pulse to the region. Another way is to select a "no phase" or "no frequency" wrap option on the scanner.

(See below and Figure 19.9)

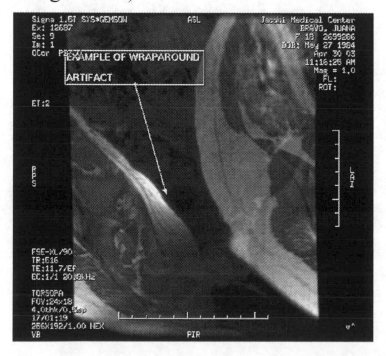

Mootoo S. Chunasamy RT (R) (CT) (MR) MSc.

TRUNCATION, GIBBS ARTIFACT, OR RING ARTIFACT

These artifacts appear as bright and dark areas of a single image. It looks like a cup shaped ring.

Solution:

Apply a raw data filter, which will smooth the edges of the image.

CHEMICAL SHIFT ARTIFACT

This is a phase difference between fat and water. It appears as a mis-mapping of signal in the frequency direction of the image, more severe when using a reduced bandwidth.

Solution:

Use a wide bandwidth.

MAGNETIC SUSCEPTIBILITY ARTIFACT

This robs the RF signal thus causing signal void on the images. Most commonly seen on gradient echo sequences.

Solution:

Shortest TE possible and smallest Voxel size. Any pulse sequence that uses 180° for re-phasing does not produce magnetic susceptibility artifact. Gradient echo does not, spin echo does. GRE uses a gradient to rephase spins therefore, magnetic susceptibility artifacts are more pronounced on the gradient echo pulse sequences.

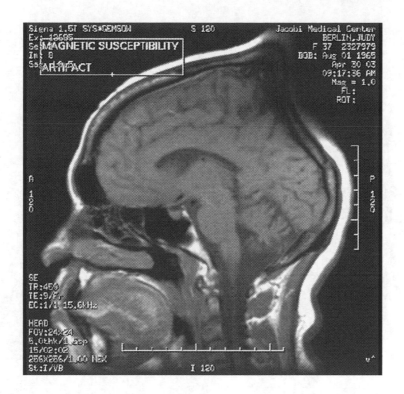

FLOW ARTIFACTS

Flow artifacts are caused by flowing blood arteries. E.g. Popliteal Artery on knees.

Solution:

Apply a Sat pulse.

PARTIAL VOLUME AVERAGING

The size of the voxel determines image resolution. The signal of different tissues is averaged mathematically. This type of artifact is caused by:

1. Slice thickness being too thick
2. Pixel size too large

11

Solution:

Decrease the field of view.

RF ARTIFACTS

This artifact is also known as zipper artifact. It is manifested as a thin, bright line along the image.

The door should be locked at all times to prevent RF interference, as this will cause RF artifacts.

CHAPTER 2

MRI SAFETY

MRI uses a very strong magnetic field to image the body. This may create dangers far more serious than the somatic effects of ionizing radiation therefore particular attention should be taken to ensure the safety of both patient and technologist. Discussed below are safety concerns in MRI imaging.

QUENCHING

The magnet is continuously cooled with liquid helium. However, if the helium level becomes excessively low, the remainder will "boil off" into the air. The following will then occur.

1. A cloud of gas will evaporate into the air
2. The magnet becomes de-magnetized
3. Patient asphyxiation and frostbite may occur
4. If a quench does occur, the technologist should evacuate the patient immediately. In order to accomplish a safe evacuation,

the technologist should enter the room by staying as close to the floor as possible and pull the patient out.

5. If a quench does occur, it takes approximately 72 hours to ramp the magnet up to full magnetic potential.

TIPS TO PREVENT QUENCHING AND PROVIDE AS SAFE AN ENVIRONMENT AS POSSIBLE IN A QUENCH SITUATION

- Maintain proper Helium levels and appropriate percentage of helium pressure as prescribed by the system manufacturer
- Continuous monitoring of "cold head" functioning by listening to chirping sounds.
- The ducts of the Air Conditioning unit should be serviced at regular intervals (no less than once per month) in order to avoid system blockages.

RF FIELDS

When a patient undergoes an MRI examination, an RF coil is attached. The nuclei of the hydrogen atoms in the body then react in a spinning motion that produces electromagnetic radiation.

CONTRAST AGENTS

FDA approved MRI contrast agents such as Gadolinium are administered at a dose of 0.1 mmol/kg or 0.2 ml/kg. Example 70 kg /patient=14ml of contrast (.1 ml per pound). There is a lethal dose, which is in excess of twenty cc per kilogram of body weight

DEFINITE CONTRAINDICATIONS FOR MRI IMAGING

- Cardiac pacemakers
- Ferrous aneurysm clips

- Cochlear Implants
- MRI magnetization will deactivate battery function and damage metallic implants within the body.

MONITORING

Ancillary devices must be MRI compatible. They must be FDA approved and tested prior to use on patients.

All patients that are sedated for MRI should be monitored. Pulse rate, oxygen level and blood pressure should be checked. An MRI compatible pulse oximeter and an MRI compatible sphygmomanometer are used. All monitors should be placed at least eight feet from isocenter for all magnets with field strengths below 3T and at least nine feet from isocenter for 3T.

LAUSTROPHOBIA

Claustrophobia is a fear of being in closed quarters. The bore of the magnet and the noise of the gradients add to claustrophobia.

Tips to prevent claustrophobia include:

1. Give clear and concise instructions to the patient
2. Provide ear plugs
3. Provide music if the MRI unit is equipped with a music system
4. Talk to the patient in-between sequences. If necessary, bring patients out of the bore of the magnet after each pulse sequence.
5. Allow a family member in the scanning room. Touching their feet during the scan is a good way to reduce claustrophobia. Reminder-All accompanying family members should be screened for contraindications

CHAPTER 3

PATIENT PREPARATION AND BASIC STEPS IN PERFORMING MRI EXAMINATIONS

PATIENT PREPARATION

1. All patients and accompanying individuals should be screened thoroughly for any possible contraindications. Documentation of the screening must be completed and retained on file for three months. Patient screening should be undertaken more than once. The patient must be initially screened at the time of the appointment, then by the referring physician and lastly by the technologist.

Although an adverse effect to a strong magnetic field or to Gadolinium will be immediate, I recommend retaining the form on file for future reference should a question arise at a later date.

2. Since the MRI is approximately 30 minutes and the magnetic environment is confining and noisy, patients should be instructed

regarding what to expect when undergoing this examination. Patients and personnel should be questioned about any metallic implants in their body. A questionnaire should be used to assure that there are no ferrous objects on the patient. This includes anyone accompanying the patient.

3. Patients should be changed into hospital gowns.
4. All jewelry should be removed including watches, rings, and chains. Credit cards, dentures, glasses, keys and especially hairpins must also be removed.
5. Explain to the patient the steps performed during the examination and what you are about to do. Tell them that the machine makes a loud noise. An excellent method of reducing fear and anxiety is to communicate with the patient in between each pulse sequence. This will ensure them that you are in close contact with them. I find this to be an effective method to gain their confidence.

BASIC STEPS IN MRI IMAGING

• STEP 1-PLAN THE EXAMINATION

Read the request carefully to determine what type of examination you are requested to perform. Know what body orientation you need to position the patient. (i.e. head first, feet first, supine or prone). Provide sponges, sheets or other devices to make the patient comfortable. For example, when performing lumbar spine imaging, provide knee sponges to straighten the lordotic curve. This will eliminate pressure from the back.

• STEP 2-RF COIL SELECTION

Select the appropriate RF coil for that particular examination. The subsequent chapters will provide suggestions regarding the use of coils for specific examination.

• STEP 3-POSITIONING

Proper positioning will eliminate the oblique planning and will result in better image quality.

• STEP 4-LANDMARK

Land marking is centering the area of interest being imaged within a specific dimension.

Landmark the part accurately. Pay particular attention to the centering of the middle of the part longitudinally. The longitudinal light must be in the midline or as close as possible to the midline. If this is not possible then use coordinates for centering. The transverse laser light must bisect the area of interest at its midpoint.

• STEP 5-PROTOCOL EXAMINATION

After positioning and land marking the patient, select the appropriate protocol to suit the examination. This protocol will differ at each institution. However, keep in mind that T_1 pulse sequences are for anatomy. T_2 sequences are for pathologies and Gradient Echoes are used wherever rapid blood flow is present. In addition, three different planes of imaging adds to the accuracy of MRI imaging.

• STEP 6-PERFORM SCOUT IMAGES AND PRESCRIPTIONING

Perform a scout or a 3-plane localizer. This refers to the Axial, Sagittal and Coronal planes. Remember, you cannot plan a sagittal from a sagittal, an axial from an axial or a coronal from a coronal. Therefore you must plan one plane from any of the other two planes. This line orientation is called a "graphic prescription".

• STEP 7-VERIFY AND DOWNLOAD PARAMETERS

Select auto prescan or manual prescan. However, with selection, the coil is tuned, the frequency is centered, and transmitted and the receiver gain is measured. If all is successful, then all parameters are downloaded. At this point scanning can commence.

If prescan fails, check the following

Hints:

1. Check body orientation
2. Correct coil selection
3. Correct coil connection

• STEP 8-ARCHIVING

Once the examination is performed successfully, make sure to save (archive) the examination on the archiving device installed with the MRI unit. In sites that have Picture Archive Communication Systems (PACS) make sure to send each examination to the appropriate designated workstation.

Make sure that the hard disc has enough space for newer examinations. Therefore, always delete old examinations to free up space. The hard disc should always be less than 50% full.

CHAPTER 4

GLOSSARIES

GLOSSARY OF LANDMARKING

Brain	Cross hair laser light at nasion. All structures of the brain at same land mark. E.g. Pituitary, IAC, Orbits, Posterior fossa.
Cervical Spine	Cross hair at C4
Thoracic Spine	Cross hair at T6
Lumbar Sacral Spine	Cross hair at 2" above the iliac crest
Chest	Mid thorax (4" above the xiphoid)
Abdomen	Cross hair at the xiphoid
Pelvis	Cross hair at the iliac crest
Hips	Cross hair at 1" below the iliac crest
Femur	Cross hair at mid femur
Knee	Cross hair at ½" below patella
Tibia/Fibula	Cross hair at mid Tibia/Fibula
Ankle	Cross hair at ankle joint
Foot	Cross hair at mid foot
Shoulder	Cross hair at 2" below the top of the shoulder

Elbow	Cross hair at elbow joint
Wrist	Cross hair at carpal bones
Hand	Cross hair at base of metacarpals

THE HUMAN SKELETAL SYSTEM

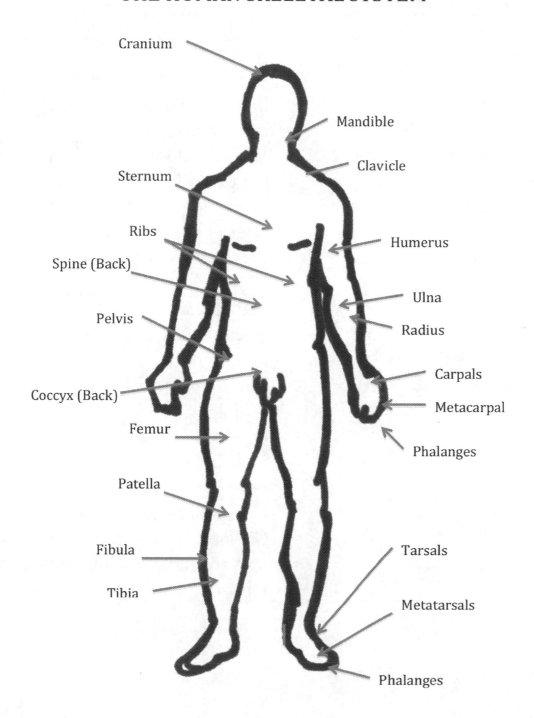

GLOSSARY OF TERMINOLOGY

TERM	ABBREV.	DEFINITION
Amplitude		The maximum value of a periodically varying quantity.
Aneurysm		Dilation of an artery
Angioma		A tumor or swelling
Artifact		A feature which appears in an image that does not belong in the imaged object.
Artifact-Wrap around	WA	When anatomy extends outside the field of view
Angiography		The imaging of veins and arteries
Atriovenous		Pertaining to both arteries and veins
Axial		A tomographic imaging plane bisecting the body into top and bottom parts
Bandwidth	RBW	The frequency at which signal is sampled
Blood brain barrier		Opposes the passage of large molecules from blood to CSF, brain or spinal tissues
Chelates		Compounds capable of binding Chelates neutralize the acidity in ions rendering Gadolinium non ionic

TERM	ABBREV.	DEFINITION
Chemical Shift		A variation in the resonance frequency of a nuclear spin due to the chemical environment around the nucleus. Chemical shift is reported in ppm
Cine		Rapid motion and functioning
Coil		Receives and transmits the RF signal
Contrast		The difference in signal intensity of two tissues in an image
Contrast Agent		A chemical substance which is introduced into an organism to change the contrast between two tissues.
Coronal		A tomographic imaging plane bisecting the body into front and back
Cryogens		Agent used in super conductive magnet to cool the coils
Demyelinating		Loss of conduction of neural impulses
Dephasing Gradient		A magnetic field gradient used to dephase transverse magnetization.
Dynamic Scanning		Rapid scanning of contrast study.
Echo		A form of magnetic resonance signal from the refocusing of transverse magnetization
Echo Planar Imaging	EPI	An MRI sequence capable of producing images at video rates.

TERM	ABBREV.	DEFINITION
Echo Time	TE	The time between the 90 degree pulse and the maximum in the echo in a spin-echo sequence
Echo Train Length	ETL	The number of 180° pulses after the 90° pulse in a fast spin echo.
Fast Spin-Echo		A multiple echo spin-echo sequence which records different regions of k-space with different echoes.
Field of View	FOV	Area of interest
Flip Angle	FA	The angle of NMV in relation to Bo. The angle and duration of the RF and how far it is tipped from longitudinal magnetization
Flux density		Magnetic winding coils
Free induction decay	FID	A form of magnetic resonance signal from the decay of transverse magnetization.
Frequency Encoding		A magnetic field gradient applied in an imaging sequence during the acquisition of a signal which encodes spins with different frequencies dependent on their position in the direction of this gradient
Functional Imaging		An imaging technique based on echo-planar imaging which is used to determine brain function
Fourier transformer	FT	Performs a mathematical conversion of analogue to digital
Gadolinium	GDPTA	MRI contrast agent

TERM	ABBREV.	DEFINITION
Gauss		Unit of measurement for the strength of a magnetic field away from isocenter
Gradient	G	A variation in some quantity with respect to another. In the context of MRI, a magnetic field gradient is a variation in the magnetic field with respect to distance
Gradient Echo		A form of magnetic resonance signal from the refocusing of transverse magnetization caused by a the application of a specific magnetic field gradient
Gradient Recalled Echo Sequence		An MRI sequence producing signals called gradient echoes as a result of the application of a refocusing echo.
Graphic Presentation		Line orientation to plan an examination in another plane
Gyriform		Rounded elevation of the brain that forms the cerebral hemisphere
Gyromagnetic Ratio		The ratio of the resonance frequency to the magnetic field strength for a given nucleus
Imaging Sequence		A specific set of RF pulses and magnetic field gradients used to produce an image.
Inferior		The direction towards the feet in an anatomical coordinate system

TERM	ABBREV.	DEFINITION
Intrathecal		Membrane that surrounds the spinal cord and cauda equina
Inversion Recovery Sequence		A pulse sequence producing signals which represent the longitudinal magnetization present after the application of a 180° inversion RF pulse
Inversion Time	Ti	The time between the inversion pulse and the sampling pulse(s) in an inversion recovery sequence
Isocenter		A location in an imaging magnet assigned the coordinates (x,y,z)=0,0,0 and having magnetic field strength Bo and resonance frequency
K-Space		That image space represented by the time and phase raw data. The Fourier transform of k-space is the magnetic resonance image
Larmor frequency		The resonance frequency of a spin in a magnetic field. The rate of precession of a spin packet in a magnetic field. The frequency which will cause a transition between the two spin energy levels of a nucleus.
Leptomeninges		Pia and Arachnoid meningeal membranes That encase the brain and spinal cord
Ligand		Capable of binding

TERM	ABBREV.	DEFINITION
LD50		Lethal dose to cause death of 50% of the exposed population
Longitudinal Magnetization	MZ	The Z component of magnetization
Magnetic Resonance Imaging	MRI	An imaging technique based on the principles of NMR
Magnitude		The length of a magnetization vector. In MRI the square root of the sum of the squares of Mx and My components of transverse magnetization.
Matrix		Rows and columns of pixels
Multiple Overlapping Thin Slice Acquisition (MOTSA)	MOTSA	Allows more than 1 slab
Net magnetic vector		Vector quantity with strength and direction
Non ionic		(Zero net charge) agents that remains neutral in water. No dissociation into ions
Pixel		Picture element
Precess		A rotational motion about an axis of a vector whose origin is fixed at the origin.
Protocol		Planes and pulse sequences to be done based on history
Pulse sequences		A set of instructions to the computer to determine how the images should look

TERM	ABBREV.	DEFINITION
Quad coil		Extremity coil
Radio Frequency	RF	Electromagnetic radiation used to stimulate protons
Relaxivity		Represents the intensity of paramagnetic agents in reducing relaxation times
Repetition Time		The time between repetitions of the basic sequence in an imaging sequence.
Resonance		An exchange of energy between two systems at a specific frequency
RF Pulse		A short burst of RF energy which has a specific shape
Sagittal		A tomographic imaging plane bisecting the body into left and right parts
Sagittal gradient	Gx	Sagittal localization at x-plane
Sampling		The time it takes to collect the signal when the readout gradient is on
Saturation pulses		A saturation band to block out signal from unwanted tissue
Shimming coils		Adds homogeneity to the B_o
Signal to noise ratio	SNR	Ratio of the amplitude of the MR signal to the amplitude of the noise
Smart Prep		Allows the use of tracking method to detect a bolus of Gadolinium

TERM	ABBREV.	DEFINITION
Specific Absorption Rate	SAR	The number of Watts of RF energy per kilogram of body weight in an imaging sequence
Spin		A fundamental property of matter responsible for MRI and NMR
Spin Density		The concentration of spins
Spin-Echo		An MRI sequence whose signal is an echo resulting from the refocusing of magnetization after the application of a 90° and 180° RF pulses
Spin-Lattice Relaxation		The return of the longitudinal magnetization to its equilibrium value along the +Z axis
Spin-Lattice Relaxation Time		The time to reduce the difference between the longitudinal magnetization and its equilibrium magnetization.
Spin-Spin Relaxation		The return of the transverse magnetization to its equilibrium value, zero
Superior		The direction towards the head in an anatomical coordinate system.
Surface Coil		An receive only RF imaging coil which, in general, fits against the surface of the object being imaged.
T_1-Weighted Image		A magnetic resonance image where the contrast is predominantly dependent on T_1

TERM	ABBREV.	DEFINITION
T_2-Weighted Image		A magnetic resonance image where the contrast is predominantly dependent on T_2
T_2^*		The spin-spin relaxation time composed of contributions from molecular interactions and inhomogeneities in the magnetic field.
Tesla	T	Unit of measurement for the strength of a magnetic field at isocenter
Tomographic		A slice with some thickness
Transverse magnetization	Mxy	The X component of the net magnetization.
Volume Imaging		Imaging which produces a three-dimensional image of an object
Voxel		Volume element

GLOSSARY OF ABBREVIATIONS

CNR	Contrast to noise ratio
CSE	Conversion spin echo
ETL	Echo train length
FA	Flip angle
FGRE	Fast gradient recalled echo
FID	Free induction delay
FS	FAT SAT
FSE	Fast spin echo
G	Gauss
GRE	Gradient recalled echo
Hz	Hertz
IR	Inversion recovery
LPPM	Line pairs per millimeter
MHz	Megahertz
mt/m	Millitesla per meter
Mxy	Transverse magnetization
Mz	Longitudinal magnetization
NEX	Number of excitations
NPW	No phase wrap
NSA	Number of signal averages
Pd	Proton density
PPM	Particles per million
RF	Radio frequency
SAT	Pre saturation pulse
SE	Spin echo
SNR	Signal to noise ratio
T	Tesla
TE	Time to echo
Ti	Inversion time
TOF	Time of flight
TR	Time to repeat
W/kg	Watts per kilogram

GLOSSARY OF BODY DIRECTIONS AND PLANES

BODY DIRECTIONS

Superior	Topmost from another part
Inferior	Below another part
Anterior	Ventral or front
Posterior	Dorsal or towards the back
Medial	Towards the center
Lateral	Towards the side
Proximal	Nearest
Distal	Farthest
Deep	Away from the surface
Superficial	Near the surface

BODY PLANES

1. Axial or Transaxial or Transverse planes divide the body into top and bottom portions.
2. Sagittal or Mid Sagittal planes divides the body into right and left halves
3. Coronal or Frontal divides the body into front and back portions

PLANES OF THE BODY

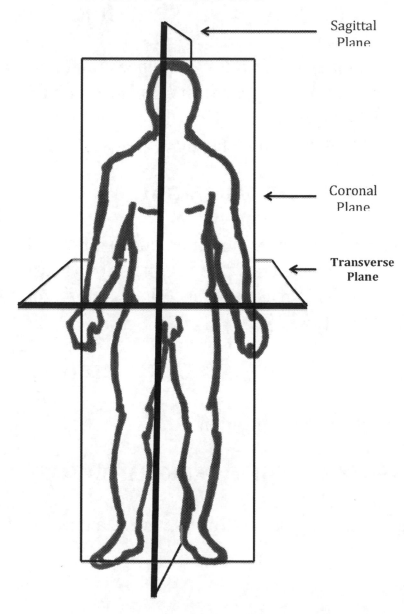

Sagittal Plane

Coronal Plane

Transverse Plane

GLOSSARY OF SCANNING ORIENTATION

H=Head
F=Feet
S=Supine
P=Prone
L=Left
R=Right

GLOSSARY OF PULSE SEQUENCES

MRI uses techniques called pulse sequences to acquire images with different tissue contrast mechanisms. Pulse sequences are a set of specific instructions programmed into the computer with an expectation as to the how the images should appear.

• DIFFUSION WEIGHTED IMAGING

Diffusion is the movement of molecules due to random thermal motion. If an incident occurs less than 72 hours prior to the scan, swelling due to edema occurs. This pulse sequence is therefore good for Cerebro Vascular Accident (CVA)

• 2 DIMENSIONAL TIME OF FLIGHT (2D TOF)

Multiple images in one acquisition

• 3 DIMENSIONAL TIME OF FLIGHT (3D TOF)

Used for faster moving blood. Covers a large atomic area

• FAST GRADIENT ECHO (FGRE)

Fast gradient imaging technique. Good wherever there is turbulent blood flow.

• SPIN ECHO (SE)

This is the most widely used pulse sequence. A spin echo pulse sequence starts with a 90° pulse and ends with a 180° pulsing.

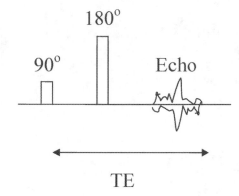

FAST SPIN ECHO (FSE)

This pulse sequence is quicker because it covers a wider range of tissue however it does increase the specific absorbed rate (SAR). FSE starts with a 90° pulse but is followed by a series of 180° pulsing

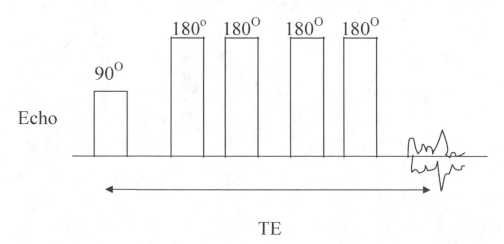

The number of 180° pulses is called the Echo Train Length (ETL). 180° pulses are used to refocus the spins.

SCAN TIME FORMULA FOR FAST SPIN ECHO:

(TR) (Number of PE) /(ETL) (NEX) / 60,000 (For time in Minutes)

<u>Example</u>

TR=3,000
Number of phase encoding=192
Echo Train Length=8
Number of excitations=2
(3,000) (192) / (8) (2) / 60,000

• INVERSION RECOVERY (IR)

This pulse sequence starts with a 180° pulse and ends with a 90° pulse. This utilizes an inversion time in addition to the TR and TE used. Inversion recovery produces T_1 weighted images.

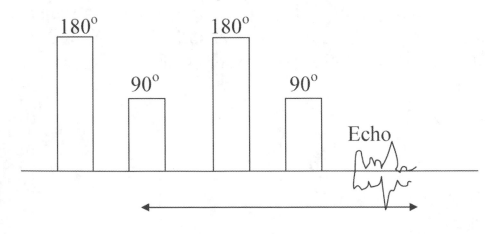

TE

• FAT SAT (FTS)

A pulse sequence used to saturate fat. This is important because fat may mask underlying pathology in areas such as the orbits or the Liver.

• FLUID ATTENUATED INVERSION RECOVERY (FLAIR)

Suppresses signal from cerebro-spinal fluid. Most applicable in the brain for seizure disorders and for spinal cord injuries. Flair utilizes a high TI.

• GRADIENT ECHOES (GRE)

A Gradient Echo uses a gradient to refocus the spins. Gradient echoes are more susceptible to blood flows. They utilize flip angles lesser than 90° in addition to TR and TE. The analogy is now different from spin echo techniques in that the higher the flips, the more T_1 related the image will be. Conversely, the lesser the flips, the more T_2 weighted the images will be.

In Spin Echo, a T_1 image is low TR and low TE. A T_2 image is high TR and high TE.

In Proton Density, the image is achieved utilizing a high TR and low TE

• LOCATOR SLICES (LOCS)

Scout views

• PHASE CONTRAST GRADIENTS (PC GRE)

Phase contrast technique used for slower flow

• SINGLE SHOT (SS)

Echo planner image with multiple slice acquisitions in quicker timing.

• FAST INVERSION RECOVERY (FIR)

Starts with $180°$ then $90°$ then a $180°$ echo train

SCAN TIME FORMULA FOR SPIN ECHO:

(TR) (Number of phase encoding) (Number of excitations) / 60,000

(For time in Minutes)

Example
TR=3,000
Number of phase encoding=192
Number of excitations=2

(3,000) (192) (2) = 1,152,000 / 60,000= 19.2 Minutes (19 minutes 12 seconds).

• SPOILED GRE RECALLED (SPGR)

Phase shifted to prevent residual trans magnetization. Decreased T_2 effects

• SHORT TAU INVERSION RECOVERY (STIR)

Suppressed signal from fat

• IN PHASE

Protons are in phase with one another

• OUT OF PHASE

Protons not being in phase with each other

• T_1

Anatomical sequence with short TR and TE

• T_1 SAGITTAL, CORONAL OR AXIAL LOCALIZER

Quick sequences performed to visualize the part being examined.

- TR of 200
- TE of 15
- NEX of .75
- Large matrix (160x128)

• T_2*

A gradient echo caused by magnetic field inhomogeneities

•T_2 PROTON DENSITY FAST SPIN ECHO AXIALS OR CORONALS

These two sequences can be done together by selecting two TE's. One short and one long.

- T_2 W is a high TR and a high TE-This is a pathological sequence
- Proton Density (PD) is a high TR and a low TE-This is an intermediate sequence, between T_1 and T_2.
  - Produces the highest contrast due to a 15% tissue differentiation.
  - Very effective PS when used in conjunjunction with fat saturation (suppression of signal from fat)

• TIME TO ECHO (TE)

The time that the echo is produced. The time between the 90° pulse and the echo.

PARTIAL SPIN ECHO

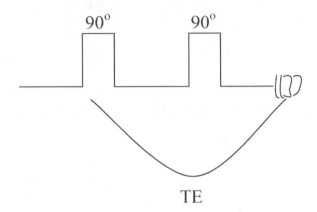

• THREE PLANE LOCALIZER (3PL LOC)

Axial, Sagittal and coronal views used for prescription.

• TIME TO REPEAT (TR)

Repetition time. The time between two 90° pulses

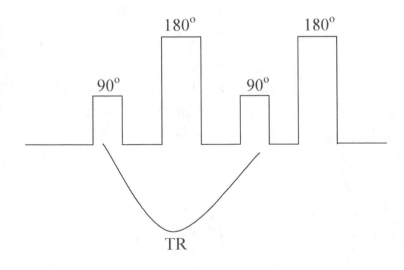

CHAPTER 5

MAGNETIC RESONANCE IMAGING OF THE BRAIN

INTRODUCTION

Magnetic Resonance Imaging is ideal for imaging the brain because of its excellent soft tissue contrast resolution. While a wide variety of chemical entities can be evaluated, (inflammatory processes, neoplasms, ischemic changes) each patient's clinical history determines the specific protocol to be used.

Certain MRI pulse sequences provide superb images of the brain. Pulse sequences are a set of instructions telling the computer how the images should look. In most instances, the history of the patient will determine the protocol to be used.

Some reasons for brain studies are:

1. Neurological deficits
2. Neurological symptoms
3. Lesions

4. Acquired Immune Deficiency syndrome (AIDS)

COIL

Head coil

Care should be taken to ensure that it slides freely along the track at the base of the coil. Connecting wires should never be looped as breakage of insulation can occur. Without insulation the exposed wire can touch the patient causing burns.

LANDMARKING

The horizontal laser light is centered at the nasion and the longitudinal light positioned through the midline of the head. The appropriate Field Of View (FOV) should be selected in order to prevent wrap around artifact. A standard FOV for most adults is 24 centimeters.

POSITIONING

The patient is positioned supine in a headfirst direction. The head is kept straight with the interpupillary line horizontal to the table. Angle sponges are placed on both sides of the head to enable proper positioning and patient comfort.

For geriatric patients and others where the neck is sometimes hyper-extended; the plane should be changed and prescribed as oblique, to obtain true axials.

SUGGESTED PROTOCOLS

1. A T_1 sagittal localizer or a coronal localizer
2. T_2/ Proton Density Fast Spin Echo axials

3. T_2/ Proton Density Fast Spin Echo coronals-Prescribed on an axial image.
4. Diffusion weighted imaging
5. Flair coronal inversion recovery

CONTRAST STUDIES

Gadolinium contrast studies are sometimes performed if a non-contrast study demonstrates a lesion. Contrast is used primarily to demonstrate enhancement or disruption of the blood brain barrier. Metastatic disease, cysticerosis and AIDS are a few clinical indications for brain studies with both pre and post gadolinium. Contrast studies must include all T_1 pulse sequences since gadolinium shortens T_1 sequences only (See figures 5.1 to 5.12).

In addition, studies of the pituitary gland, orbits, posterior fossa and internal auditory canal, should always be done pre and post gadolinium with thin sections. When imaging the pituitary gland, dynamic studies must be done to visualize the stalk of the pituitary gland for micro adenomas.

- For orbital imaging-Pre and post FAT SAT axials and coronals in addition to the routine brain protocol (See figures 5.13 to 5.18).
- For pituitary imaging-After administering gadolinium, imaging in the coronal plane should be done first (See figures 5.21 to 5.25).

In case of post trauma patients with suspected bleeding of the brain, a gradient echo T_2 coronal is the pulse sequence of choice.

This is mainly because Gradient Echo sequences are more susceptible to blood flow.

Figure 5-1　　　　　　　**SAGITTAL LOCALIZER FOR AXIAL PLANE**

This is a Sagittal plane. The lines are placed transversely. This orientation will produce axial slices (see figure 5-5).

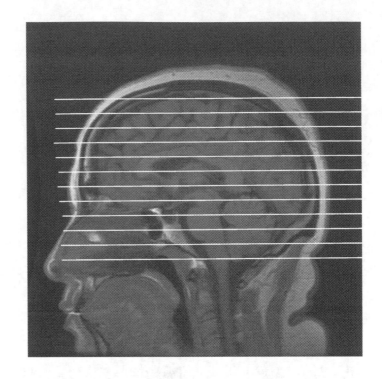

Figure 5-2　　　　　　　T_1 **SAGITTAL WITHOUT GADOLINIUM**

This is a T_1 image. It displays much anatomy and fat is hyperintense.

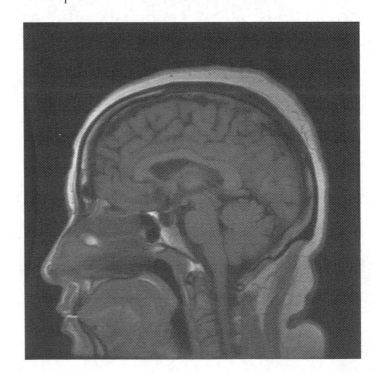

Figure 5-3   **DIFFUSION AXIAL PLANNING**

This is a Sagittal image.
The lines are axial
prescription timing
but the pulse sequence
is diffusion. Done to
visualize an infarct. It is
an EPI pulse sequence
(see figure 5-7)

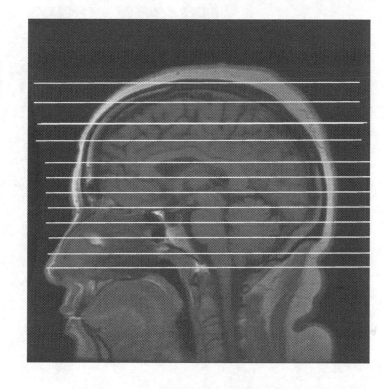

Figure 5-4   **CORONAL PLANNING**

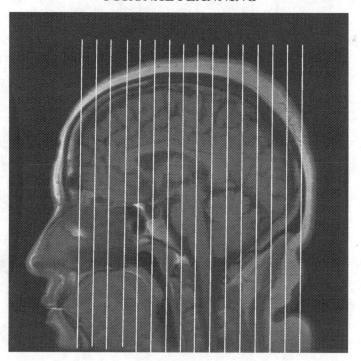

Figure 5-5   **T₂W AXIAL**

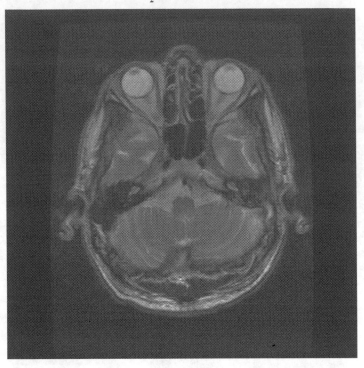

Figure 5-6   **T₁W CORONAL**

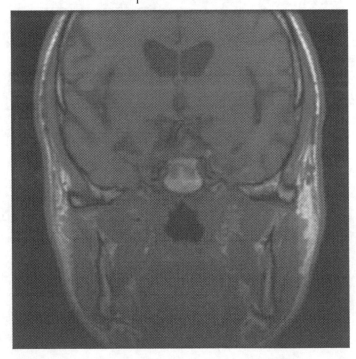

Figure 5-7

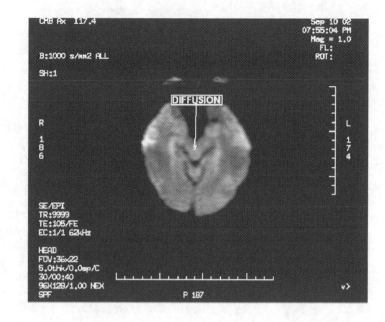

This is a diffusion
image.
An EPI sequence. Uses
a B-value of 1000. Good
for brain and body
studies.

Figures 5-8

CONTRAST   **NON CONTRAST**

These are Sagittal
images with and without
contrast.
A good sign of contrast
in the brain is Dural
sinus fillings

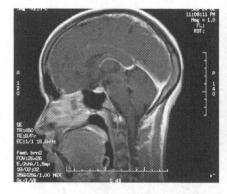 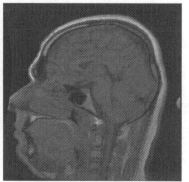

Figure 5-9

Axial image is a result
of figure 5-3

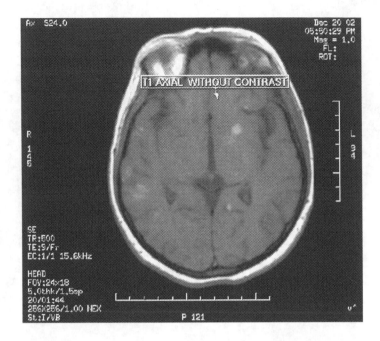

Figure 5-10

Same image as 5-9 but
notice this with contrast

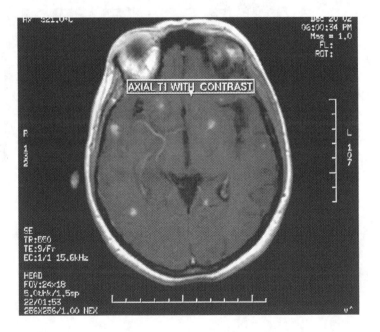

Figure 5-11

Axial T_1 image with contrast. T_1 sequences are always done after contrast because of low TR or low TE and the quicker tissue return back to equilibrium and the brighter signal

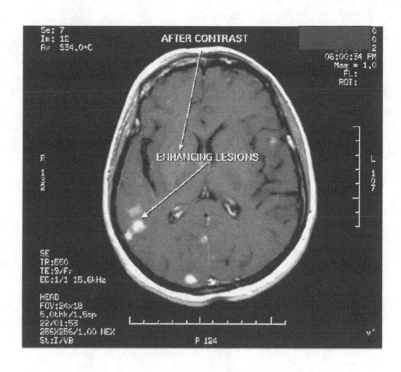

Figure 5-12

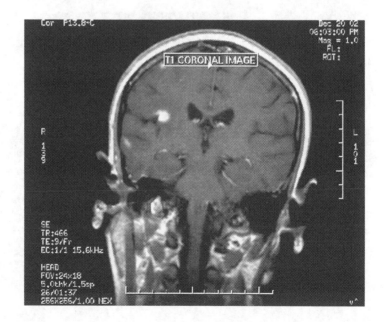

Figure 5-13

This is a Sagittal image. The lines are showing how to prescribe orbital studies

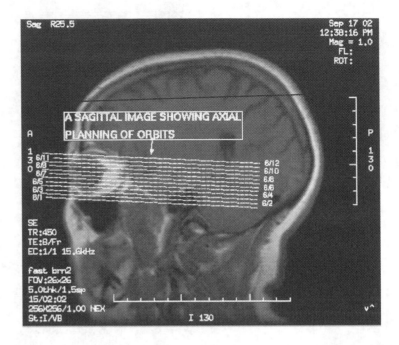

Figure 5-14

AXIAL T₁ OF ORBITS

This is an Axial T₁ image of the orbits. It is the result of figure 5-13- non Fat Sat

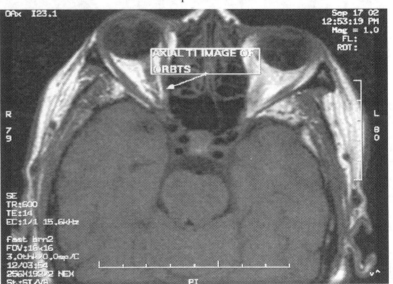

Figure 5-15   **AXIAL WITH FAT SAT**

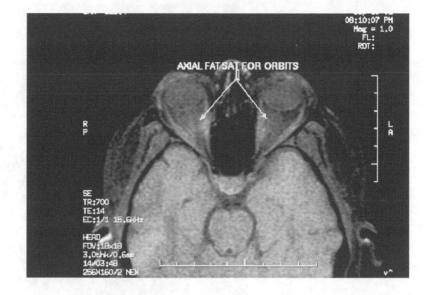

This is an Axial image
of the orbits. It is with
Fat Sat. This is a result
of figure 5-13

Figure 5-16

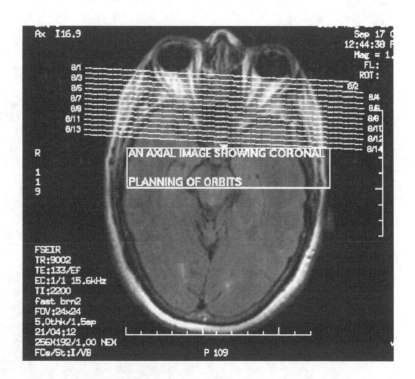

This is an Axial image.
The lines are placed
anterior to poster to
cover the optic chiasm
for Coronal slices (see
figure 5-17).

Figure 5-17   **CORONAL FAT SAT**

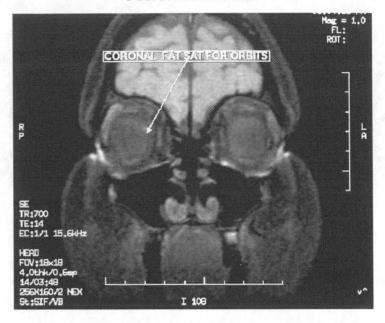

This is a Coronal Fat Sat
image without contrast

Figure 5-18   **T₁W AXIAL FAT SAT WITH CONTRAST OF ORBITS**

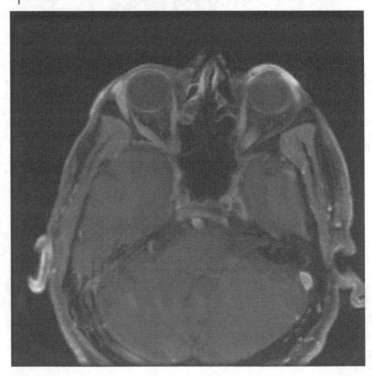

T₁ Fat Sat of orbits

Figure 5-19

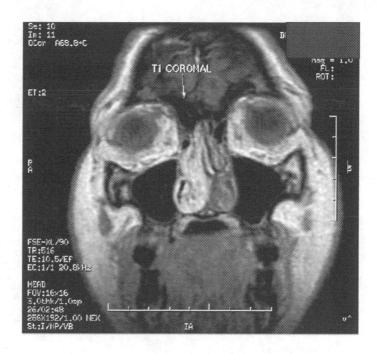

T_1 Coronal. No Fat Sat.

Figure 5-20   **T_1W CORONAL FAT SAT WITH CONTRAST OF ORBITS**

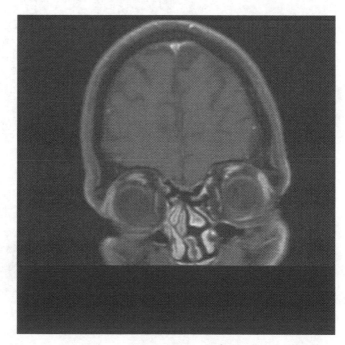

T_1 Coronal with Fat Sat.

Figure 5-21

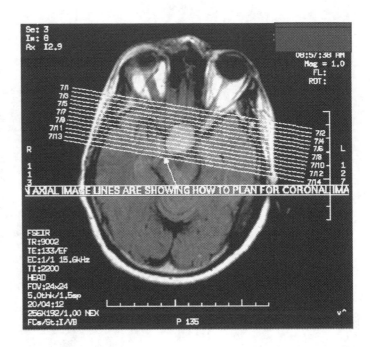

Pituitary Gland study.
Prescription lines will
result in Coronal images
(see figure 5-23).

Figure 5-22

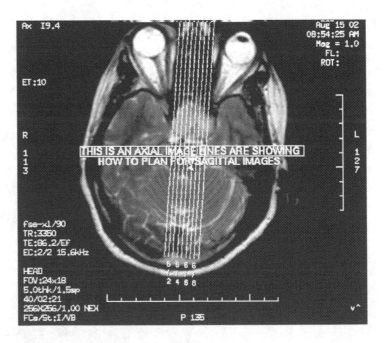

This is an Axial image.
Prescription lines are
showing how to obtain
a Sagittal image figure
5-24).

Figure 5-23

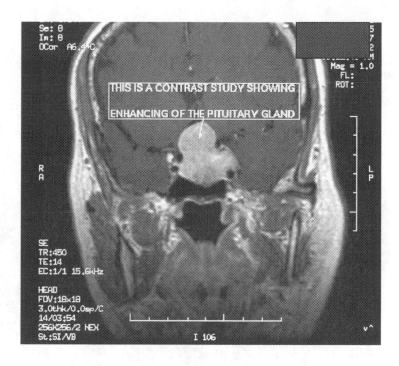

This is a T$_1$ Coronal image demonstrating a large tumor.

Figure 5-24

T$_1$W SAGITTAL WITHOUT CONTRAST

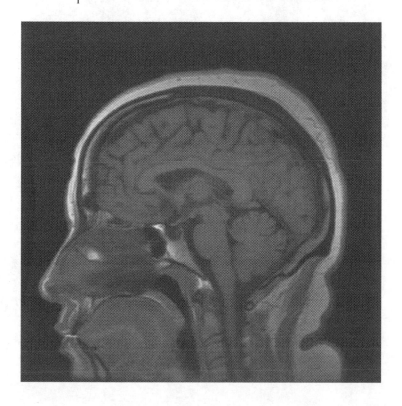

Figure 5-25   **T₁ SAGITTAL OF PITUITARY GLAND WITH CONTRAST**

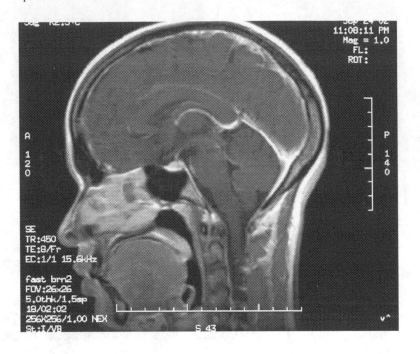

CHAPTER 6

MRA IMAGING OF THE BRAIN

In addition to imaging the tissues of the brain, MRA can be performed non-invasively, to visualize the Circle of Willis

CLINICAL INDICATIONS FOR MRA OF THE BRAIN

1. Un-ruptured aneurysm
2. Atrioventricular Malformation (AVM)
3. Arterial occlusion and stenosis

COIL

The head coil is used for MRA of the head.

LANDMARK

The longitudinal light is at the midline of the head. The horizontal light is at the nasion.

POSITIONING

The patient is supine with the head very straight. Side sponges are placed to secure the head.

SUGGESTED PROTOCOL

3D TOF is employed to visualize fast moving blood. Its application to image the Circle of Willis produces excellent images (See figures 6.2 to 6.6).

Gradient moment nulling and magnetization transfer techniques are applied to suppress all background stationary tissues thereby leaving flowing blood very bright.

Saturation pulses are used with positioning in such a way as to block out inflow from irrelevant vessels. This 3D TOF phenomenon utilizes no gap. It is one thick slab with multiple acquisitions.

In addition, a technique called MOTSA (Multiple Overlapping Thin Slice Acquisition) can also be used to cover a wider area of the brain (See figure 6.1).

1-SLAB

MOTSA

From the maximum projection image, reconstruction is performed to segregate the posterior, right and left sections of the Circle of Willis to facilitate better resolution and makes it easier for the radiologist to interpret.

MRA OF CIRCLE OF WILLIS

Figure 6-1   **T$_1$ SAGITTAL ILLUSTRATING MRA PRESCRIPTION**

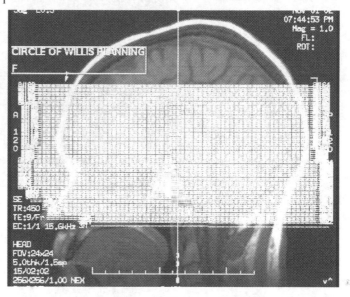

Figure 6-2

CIRCLE OF WILLIS IN ITS ENTIRETY
MAXIMUM INTENSITY PROJECTION (MIP) IMAGE

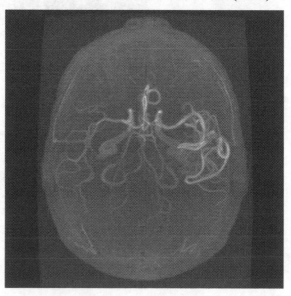

Figure 6-3   **IVI AFTER RECONSTRUCTION**
OF RIGHT SIDE OF CIRCLE OF WILLIS

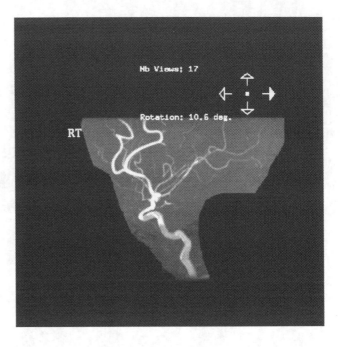

Figure 6-4   **IVI AFTER RECONSTRUCTION**
OF LEFT SIDE OF CIRCLE OF WILLIS

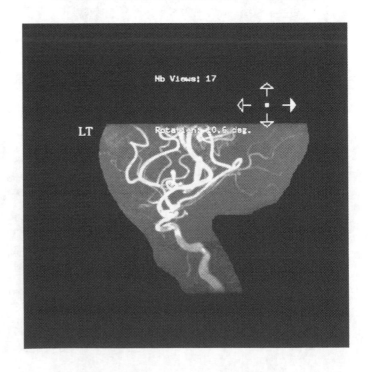

Figure 6-5   **POSTERIOR CIRCULATION OF CIRCLE OF WILLIS**

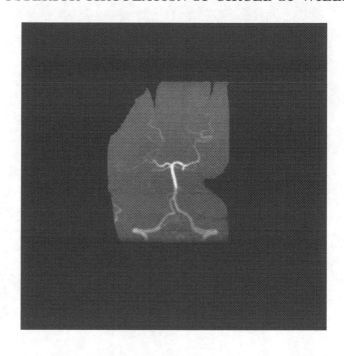

Figure 6-6   **ENTIRE CIRCLE OF WILLIS AFTER RECONSTRUCTION**

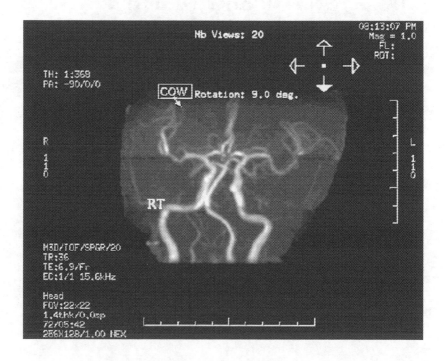

CHAPTER 7

MAGNETIC RESONANCE VENOGRAPHY (MRV) OF THE BRAIN

INDICATION FOR MRV OF THE BRAIN

Superior sagittal sinus thrombosis

COIL

The dedicated head coil is used. This is a tranceive coil capable of both transmitting and receiving radio frequency signals.

LAND MARKING

The horizontal laser light is crossing the nasion. The longitudinal laser light is passing the midline of the head.

POSITIONING

The patient is supine with the head very straight. Small rectangular sponges are provided on both sides of the head to maintain good positioning.

SUGGESTED PROTOCOL

1. A T_1 sagittal scan is performed first
2. T2 Ax/PD FSE
3. Flair axial FSE IR
4. Coronal 2D TOF SPGR
5. Sagittal PC GRE venous

In addition to the MRV a routine brain study is performed

Coronal 2D TOF SPGR

From the sagittal sequence, select a mid slice and prescribe the above sequence. Care must be taken to start above the cortex of the head to the base of the skull.

IMPORTANT:

The saturation band must be placed inferiorly in order to prevent arterial blood from going up to the brain (See figure 7.1).

All the other pulse sequences are done using the same protocols as a routine brain MRI

Mootoo S. Chunasamy RT (R) (CT) (MR) MSc.

Figure 7-1   **MRV OF THE BRAIN**

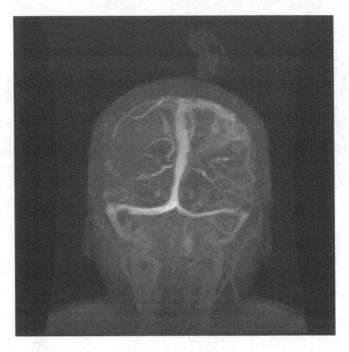

CHAPTER 8

SCANNING THE SPINE

SCANNING THE CERVICAL SPINE

INDICATIONS FOR CERVICAL SPINE SCANNING

1. Cervical cord compression
2. Spinal infection
3. Spinal tumor
4. Brain stem disease
5. Syrinx
6. Multiple sclerosis
7. Cervicolagia

COIL

CTL phased array coil is best for this examination. This is a contraption whereby many coils are plugged into one to produce the image. The quadrature or anterior commissure coil can also be used.

65

LAND MARKING

The horizontal laser light is parallel to C4 and the longitudinal light is at the midline of the neck.

PATIENT POSITIONING

The patient is lying supine, head first. The neck must be very straight.

The patient is instructed not to swallow at the time of scanning. However; in between each pulse sequence the patient may swallow.

SUGGESTED PROTOCOL

1. A 3 plane localizer (scout) FGRE
2. T_1 sagittal (low TR, low TE) SE
3. T_2 sagittal (high TR, High TE) FSE
4. T_2 gradient echo axials

In case of tumors perform:

> Post contrast T_1 sagittal SE
> T_1 axials SE

In case of trauma perform:

Stir sagittals and axials

Note: Trans axials are prescribed in such a way that the lines are placed parallel to the intervertebral disc space.

All planes are prescribed so as to cover from C-1 to C-7.

SOFT TISSUE NECK

Typical cervical spine positioning is applied. The same coils and land marking are used. The only difference is in the protocol. Fat Saturation pulse sequences are used.

All soft tissue examinations are done pre and post gadolinium. Since Gadolinium shortens the T_1 pulses sequences, post gadolinium T_1 sagittals and axials are done (See figures 8.1-8.7).

SCANNING THE THORACIC SPINE

INDICATIONS FOR THORACIC SPINE IMAGING

1. Spinal cord compression
2. Syrinx
3. Abscess
4. Osteomyelitis
5. Herniation of the nucleus pulposis
6. To evaluate for Metastatic disease

COIL

As in the cervical spine, the CTL coil is used.

LAND MARKING

The horizontal laser light is parallel to the T-4 area. Use a large FOV in order to include the C-2 vertebra. This will allow the radiologist to count downwards. A sagittal localizer should be performed for this reason only.

In addition a coronal localizer should be done.

POSITIONING

The patient is lying supine, head first. The body is very straight.

SUGGESTED PROTOCOL

1. A 3 plane localizer is performed
2. Sagittal T_1 SE
3. Sagittal T_2 FSE

If any pathology is seen than axial slices are prescribed to cover the affected area. Otherwise, axials are not routinely performed.

In trauma patients, STIR images are added.

If a tumor is seen, then post gadolinium T_1 sequences are performed in the axial and sagittal planes.

NOTE: Gibbs or truncation artifact are common in the thoracic area. This looks like splitting of the spinal cord. This artifact mimics a syrinx (See figures 8.8 to 8.15).

LUMBAR SACRAL SPINE

INDICATIONS FOR LUMBAR SPINE SCANNING

1. Spinal cord compression
2. Syrinx
3. Abscess
4. Osteomyelitis
5. Herniation of the nucleus pulposis
6. To evaluate for Metastatic disease

COIL

The phased array coil is used

LAND MARKING

The horizontal laser light is about 2" above and parallel to the Iliac Crest. The longitudinal light is at the center of the midline of the body.

POSITIONING

The patient is lying supine, headfirst and the body is very straight. Provide a foam pad under the knees to relieve pressure from the back by straightening the lordotic curve.

SUGGESTED PROTOCOL

1. A 3 plane localizer is performed
2. T_1 SE sagittal
3. T_2 FSE sagittal
4. T_1 FSE axials-parallel to the disc space
5. T_2 FSE axials parallel to the disc space.

To rule out cancer, abscesses and Osteomyelitis do pre and post gadolinium-T_1 sagittals and T_1 axials.

NOTE: All post operative spinal studies must be done with Gadolinium. This is mainly done in order to differentiate scar tissue from normal disc.

Scanning must be done within twenty minutes after the administration of Gadolinium (See figures 8.16 to 8.21).

CORONAL IMAGE
THE LINE ORIENTATION SHOWS HOW
TO PLAN FOR SAGITTAL IMAGES

Figure 8-1

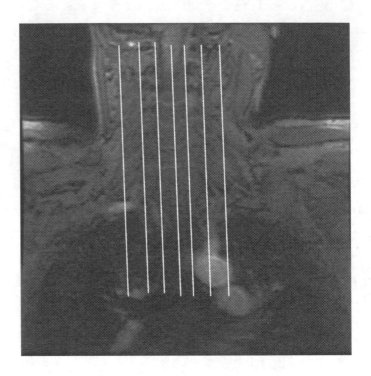

SAGITTAL IMAGE
THE LINE ORIENTATION SHOWS HOW TO PLAN
FOR AXIAL IMAGES

Figure 8-2

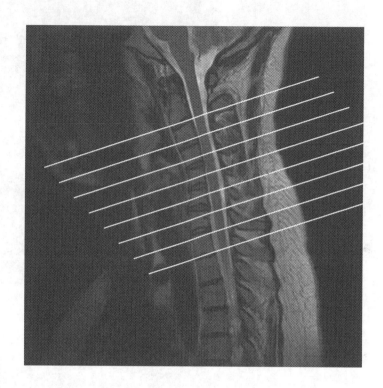

Figure 8-3

T₁W SAGITTAL IMAGE

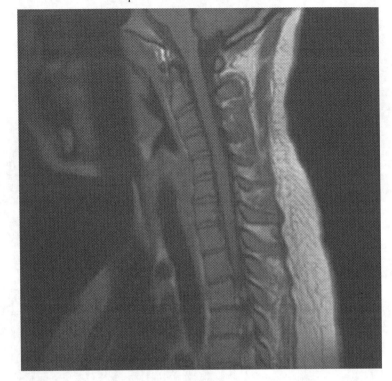

T₂ Sagittal image. Note that the spinal cord is hyperdense in comparison to Cerebral Spinal Fluid.

Figure 8-4

T₂W SAGITTAL IMAGE

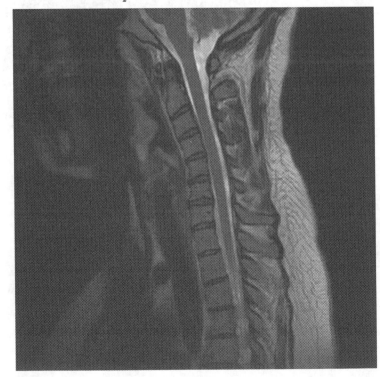

T₂ Sagittal image. Note that the spinal cord is hypodense in comparison to Cerebral Spinal Fluid.

Figure 8-5

T₂ SAGITTAL IMAGE

T_2 Sagittal image demonstrating a C7 fracture

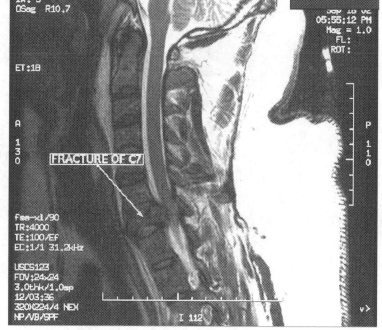
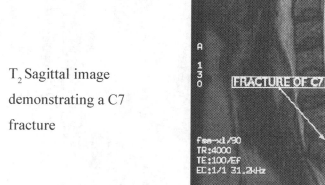

Figure 8-6

T₁W SAGITTAL IMAGE

T_1 W Sagittal image demonstrating multiple disc herniations

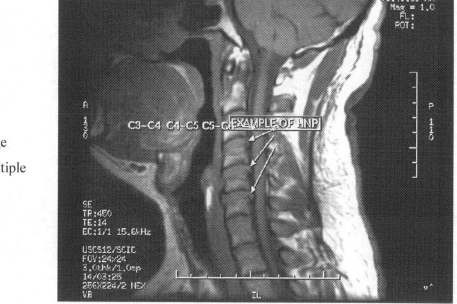

Figure 8-7

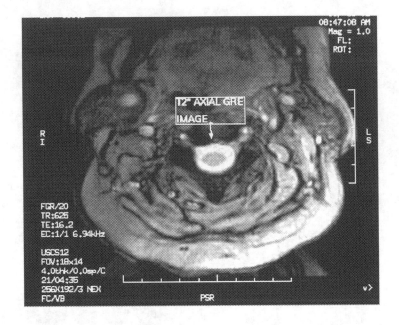

T_2^* GRE image. Best to visualize nerve roots

Figure 8-8

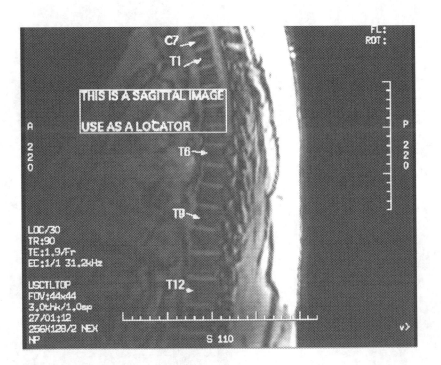

Figure 8-9   **CORONAL LOCALIZER SHOWING T$_2$ SAGITTAL**
PLANNING

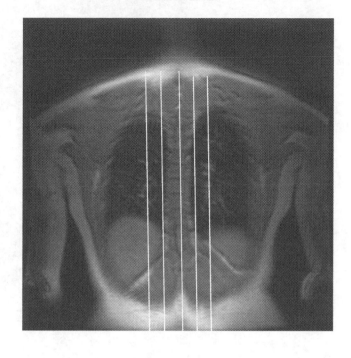

Figure 8-10   **CORONAL LOCALIZER SHOWING T$_1$ SAGITTAL**
PLANNING

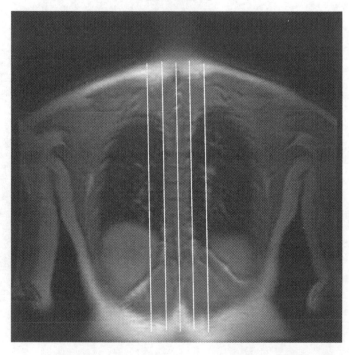

Figure 8-11

T₂W SAGITTAL IMAGE

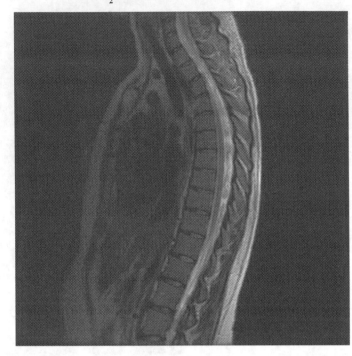

This is a result of figure
8-9 prescriptioning

Figure 8-12

T₁W SAGITTAL IMAGE

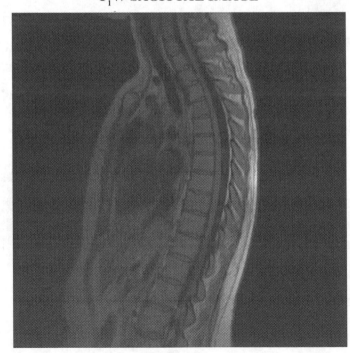

This is a result of figure
8-10 prescriptioning

Figure 8-13

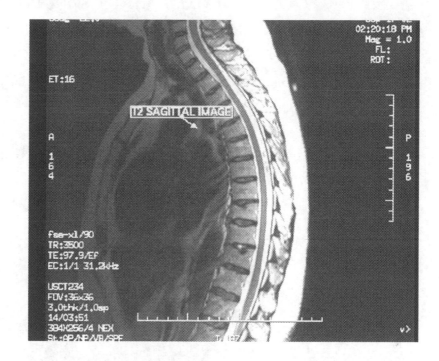

Figure 8-14   **SAGITTAL OF CERVICAL AND THORACIC SPINE**

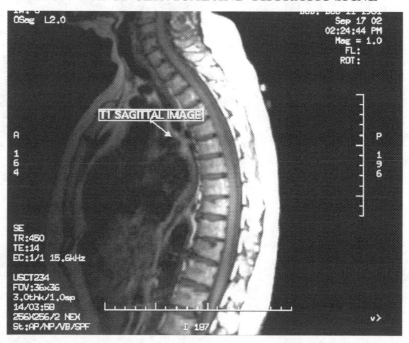

AXIAL THORACIC SPINE CORONAL IMAGE

Figure 8-15
LINE ORIENTATION IS SHOWING HOW TO PLAN FOR
SAGITTAL IMAGES

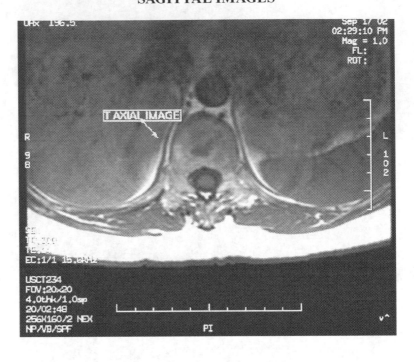

SAGITTAL IMAGE

Figure 8-16
LINE ORIENTATION IS SHOWING HOW TO PLAN
TRANSAXIALS

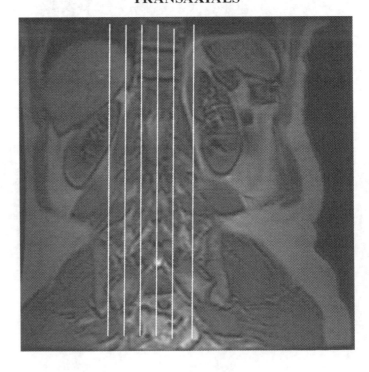

SAGITTAL IMAGE

Figure 8-17

LINE ORIENTATION IS SHOWING HOW TO PLAN

TRANSAXIALS

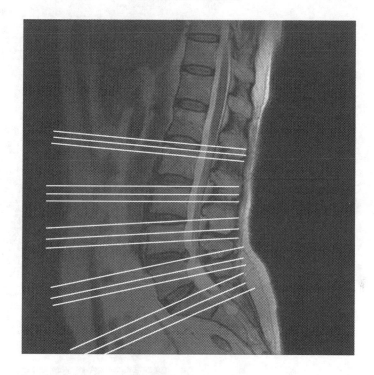

This Sagittal image
demonstrates HNP of
L4 L5 area

Figure 8-18

T$_2$ SAGITTAL IMAGE

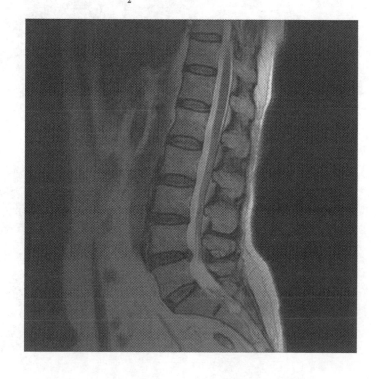

79

Figure 8-19   **T₁ SAGITTAL IMAGE**

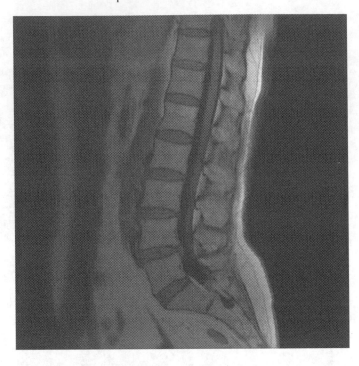

Figure 8-20   **T₂ AXIAL IMAGE**

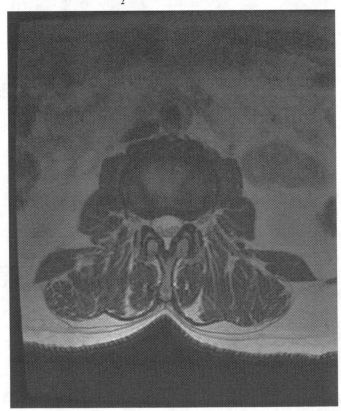

A result of figure 8-17
prescription

Figure 8-21

T₁ AXIAL IMAGE

A result of figure 8-17
prescription

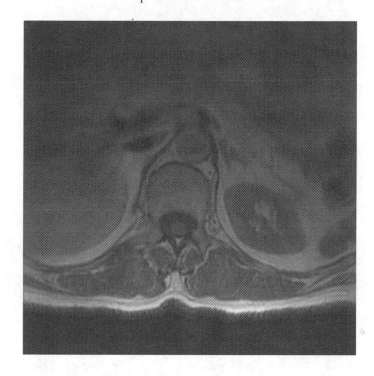

CHAPTER 9

MAGNETIC RESONANCE ANGIOGRAPHY

HOW TO PERFORM MRA OF THE CAROTID ARTERIES

SOME INDICATIONS FOR PERFORMING AN
MRA OF THE CAROTID ARTERIES:

1. Rule out CVA
2. Abnormal Ultrasound

COIL

The phased array Neurovascular coil is used

LAND MARKING

The longitudinal laser light is at the midline of the neck. The horizontal laser light is crossing at the chin.

POSITIONING

The patient is supine headfirst. The head is kept very straight and taped down. The patient is instructed to listen for breathing instructions.

SUGGESTED PROTOCOL

1. 3 plane T_2* FGRE localizer is performed
2. A sagittal phase contrast GRE
3. Axial locator slices to identify the carotids are performed at the level of C4. Do about six slices
4. 2D TOF axial SPGR
5. 3D TOF coronal SPGR

The power injector is loaded with Gadolinium in barrel "A". In sites that have a double barrel syringe injector, normal saline is loaded in the other syringe designated as barrel "B". Before starting the examination, an angiocath is placed, preferably in the antecubital vein. Make sure that the angiocath is secured with an Opsite. On the injector control located on the outside by the scanning console, set a pressure rate of about 1.5 to 2.5 ml/sec. In patients with very small veins a lower flow rate is desired.

PRE TUNING

This is the process of adjusting transmit and receiver gain to obtain optimum signal to noise ratio at the Lamar equation

AXIAL LOCATOR

From the 3-plane localizer, select a sagittal image and plan six slices at the level of C4.

SAGITTAL PC GRE

From the 3-plane localizer chose an axial slice that demonstrates the carotid arteries. The prescribed line, which is only one slice, is placed directly on the carotid artery. See resultant image Figure 9-1

2D TOF AXIAL SPGR

From the sagittal PC image, prescribe the axials starting from the aorta to the bifurcation of the carotids. See figure 9-3.

TOF CORONAL SPGR

Again from the sagittal PC, place the slab to cover the carotids from the base of the aorta to the bifurcation. Then a tracker is placed on one of the axial locators depicting the carotid artery. When clicked on the word "tracker", the cursor will be like this:

Reduce the size to the roundness of the carotids. E.g. Carotid artery

Cursor

At this point, make sure to enter the amount and type of contrast used.

"Smart Prep" is employed. The power injector is armed making sure all air is expelled. The message center on the scan monitor is cleared and "Prep Scan" is performed. After the pre scan is complete, the machine will ask to start the scan. Press start scan and watch the message area which will say "acquiring baseline" then that will change to say "begin injection" Tell the patient to stop breathing and start the injection immediately.

Smart Prep 3D TOF for carotid should be programmed in such a way so as the time must be less than 30 seconds See figures .1 to 9.10).

2 D MRA OF THE CAROTID ARTERIES WITHOUT GADOLINIUM

Figure 9-1

THIS IS AN AXIAL

2 D MIP IMAGE (ALSO KNOWN AS SOURCE IMAGE)

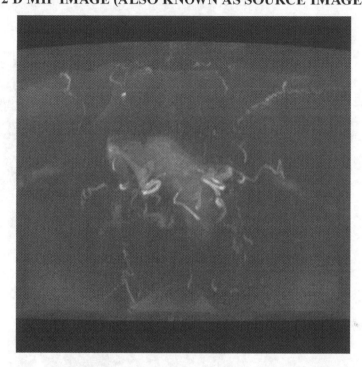

Figure 9-2

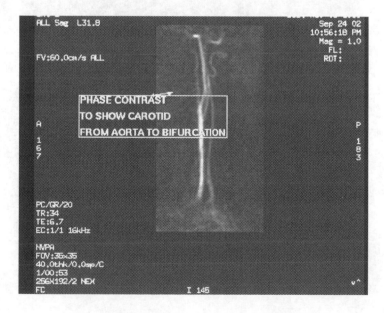

3PHASE CONTRAST IMAGE

Figure 9-3   **DEMONSTRATING CAROTID ARTERY FROM THE AORTA TO THE BIFURCATION**

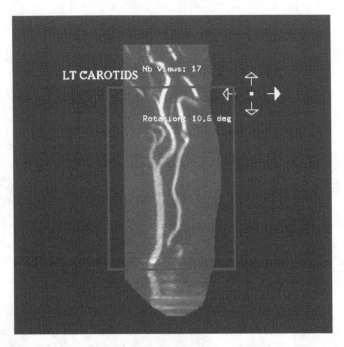

Figure 9-4   **2 D MIP IMAGE OF CAROTID ARTERIES WITHOUT CONTRAST**

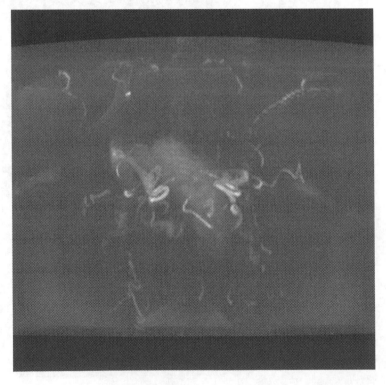

Figure 9-5 **2 D TOF WITHOUT CONTRAST**

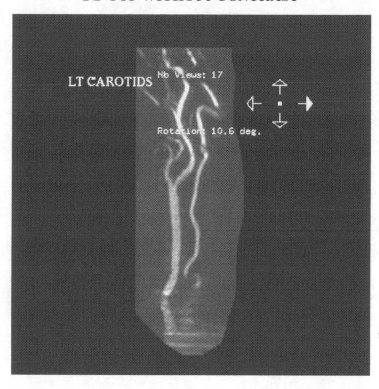

Figure 9-6 **2 D TOF WITHOUT CONTRAST**

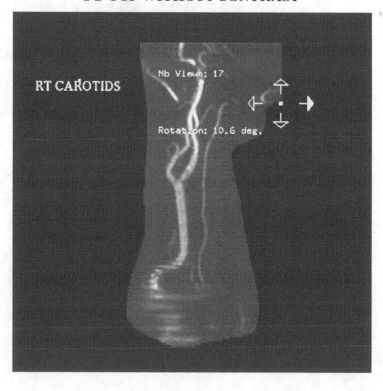

Figure 9-7   **SAGITTAL PHASE CONTRAST IMAGE ILLUSTRATING 3 D**
TIME OF FLIGHT PRESCRIPTION WITH CONTRAST

A result of figure
9-7 prescription

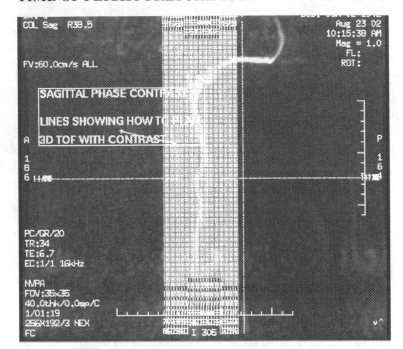

Figure 9-8   **3 D TOF WITH CONTRAST**

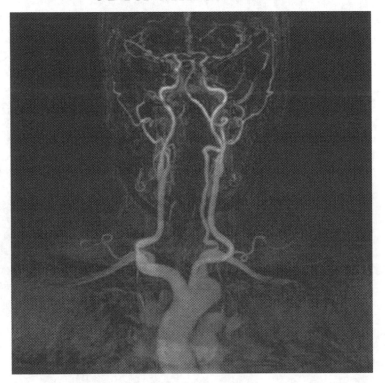

Figure 9-9   **LEFT RECONSTRUCTION IMAGE OF CAROTID ARTERY**

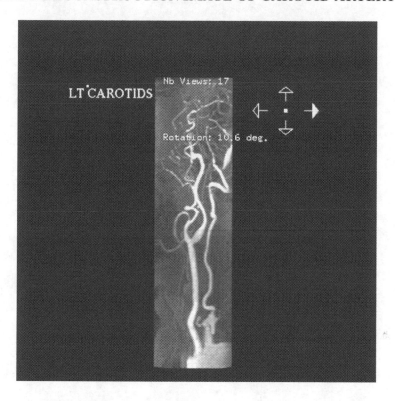

Figure 9-10   **RIGHT RECONCSTRUCTION IMAGE OF CAROTID ARTERY**

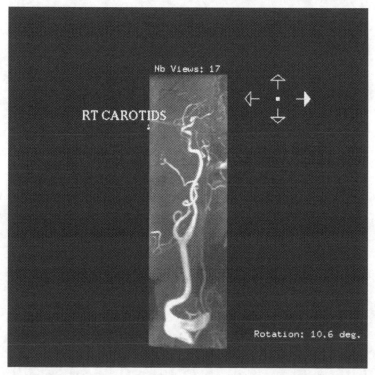

CHAPTER 10

SCANNING THE SHOULDER

INDICATIONS FOR SHOULDER SCANNING

1. Shoulder pain
2. Impingement
3. Instability
4. Rotator cuff tear
5. Cysts

COIL

The dedicated phased array shoulder coil is the best for shoulder imaging.

LAND MARKING

The longitudinal laser light is as close as possible to the center of the shoulder being imaged while the transverse laser light is bisecting the mid-humeral head. It is important to set an offset if the affected shoulder is too far off from the center. For example, if the right side is being examined, an offset of R80 is set so that the image will move as close as possible to center.

POSITIONING

The patient is supine, headfirst. The shoulder should be flat on the table with the hand supinated. It is necessary to turn the patient approximately 15^0 towards the affected side. In order to obtain a true coronal image.

A 3 plane localizer is performed utilizing a T_2* FGRE pulse sequence.

SUGGESTED PROTOCOL

1. Axial PD gradient echo
2. Axial FSE Pd FAT SAT
3. Oblique Coronal T_2 FSE
4. Oblique Coronal IR
5. Oblique Sagittal FSE

A. When performing the axial gradient echo, use a coronal image and prescribe from the superior aspect of the gleno-humeral head to the inferior aspect of the gleno-humeral head (See figure 10.1).
B. When prescribing the oblique coronal use the mid axial slice. This slice looks like an ice cream cone. The lines are placed in such a way that they are perpendicular to the glenoid fossa (See figure 10.2).
C. The oblique coronal is also prescribed the same as the above.
D. When prescribing the sagittal T_1 FSE, the orientation of the lines are now placed parallel to the glenoid fossa. Make sure to include the Supraspinatus muscle (See figure 10.3).

Proper prescription pertaining to angulation when planning coronals must be maintained otherwise the image will be flipped to the opposite shoulder.

(See figures 10.1 to 10.8)

HOW TO SCAN A SHOULDER
HOW TO GET AN AXIAL IMAGE

Figure 10-1   **USE A CORONAL IMAGE AND PRESCRIBE FROM THE SUPERIOR ASPECT OF THE GLENO-HUMERAL HEAD TO THE INFERIOR ASPECT OF THE GLENO-HUMERAL HEAD**

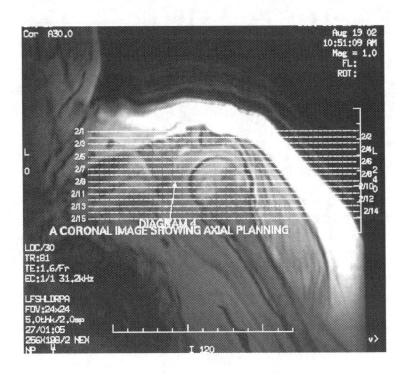

Figure 10-2   USE THE MID AXIAL SLICE. THE LINES ARE PLACED IN
SUCH A WAY THAT THEY ARE PERPENDICULAR TO THE
GLENOID FOSSA

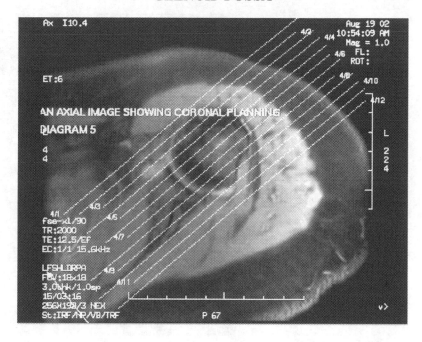

Figure 10-3   THE SAGITTAL T₁ FSE, THE ORIENTATION OF THE LINES
ARE NOW PLACED PARALLEL TO THE GLENOID FOSSA.
MAKE SURE TO INCLUDE THE SUPRASPINATUS MUSCLE

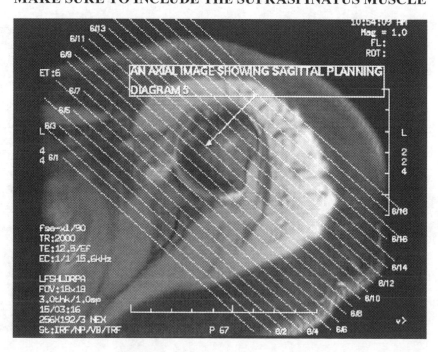

HOW TO GET A "GRADIENT" AXIAL IMAGE

Figure 10-4   **THIS IS THE RESULT OF THE FIGURE 10-1 PRESCRIPTION**

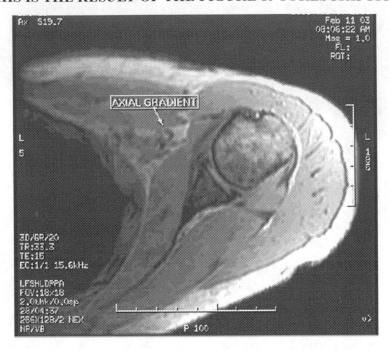

HOW TO GET A "STIR" AXIAL IMAGE

Figure 10-5   **THIS IS THE RESULT OF THE FIGURE 10-2 PRESCRIPTION**

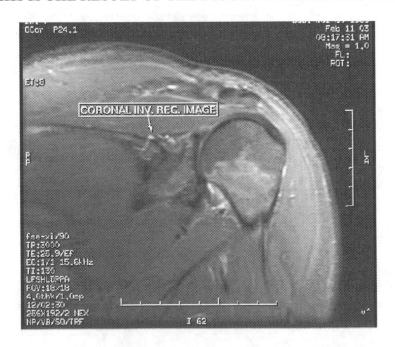

Figure 10-6   **HOW TO GET A "CORONAL T$_1$" AXIAL IMAGE**

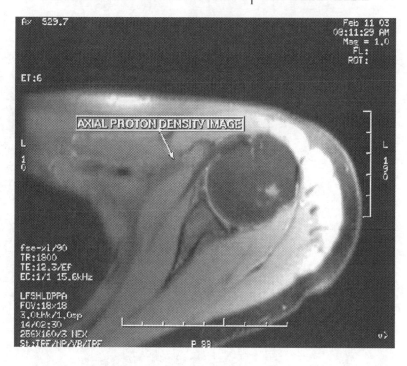

Figure 10-7   **THIS IS THE RESULT OF THE FIGURE 10-2 PRESCRIPTION**

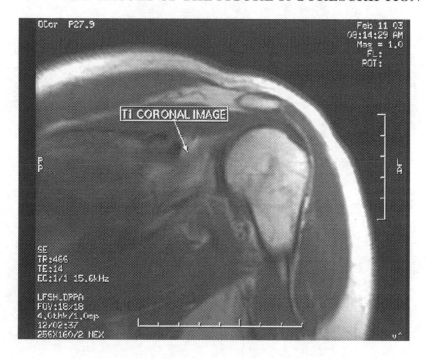

HOW TO GET A "SAGITTAL T$_1$" AXIAL IMAGE

Figure 10-8   **THIS IS THE RESULT OF THE FIGURE 10-3 PRESCRIPTION**

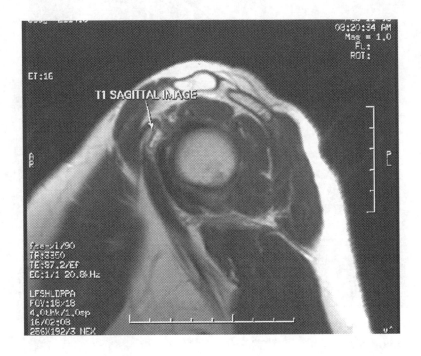

CHAPTER 11

SCANNING THE ELBOW

INDICATIONS

1. Trauma
2. Nerve compression
3. Frozen or locked elbow

COIL

The quad extremity coil or dedicated elbow coil or flex coil is used

LANDMARKING

The longitudinal laser light is at the midline of the elbow. The horizontal light is crossing exactly at the elbow joint.

POSITIONING

The patient is lying prone with the headfirst. The hand is supinated and supported with sponges for patient comfort.

SUGGESTED PROTOCOL

A three plane localizer is performed utilizing a C-T_2^*F.

1. T_2 axial FSE
2. T_1 coronal SE
3. Coronal T_2 FS, Coronal 2D GRE
4. Sagittal Stir

(See figures 11.6 to 11.11)

5. If contrast is indicated than the following is suggested:
   a. T_1 Axial FS
   b. T_1 Sagittal FS
   c. T_1 Coronal FS

T_2 AXIAL FSE

From the localizer images, select a mid coronal image and prescribe axial sliced from top to bottom to cover to cover the elbow joint (see figure 11.1)

T_1 CORONAL AND CORONAL IR

From the localizer series, select a mid sagittal image and prescribe anterior to posterior slices (see figure 11-3).

SAGITTAL IR

From the localizer series, select a mid coronal image and prescribe slices running from left to right (see figure 11-4)

AXIAL PRESCRIPTIONING

Figure 11-1

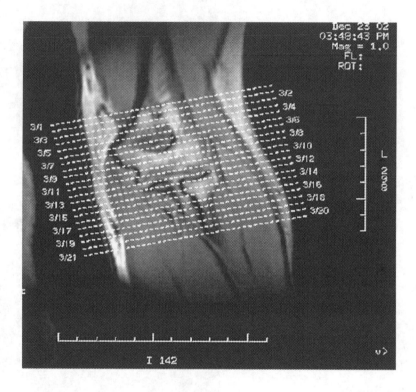

Figure 11-2   SAGITTAL PRESCRIPTIONING

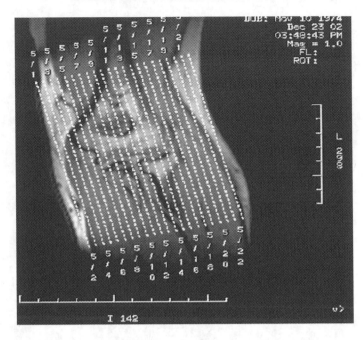

Figure 11-3   SAGITTAL PRESCIPTIONING

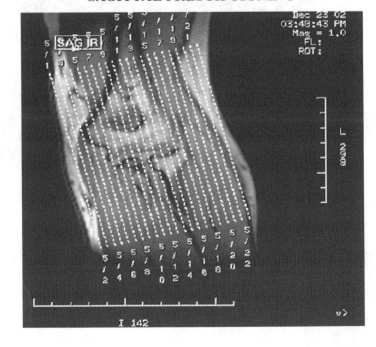

A result of figure 11-1

prescriptioning

Figure 11-4   **CORONAL PRESCRIPTIONING**

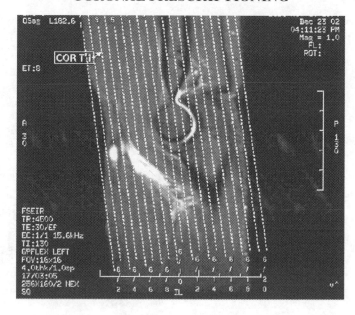

Figure 11-5   **T$_1$ AXIAL IMAGE**

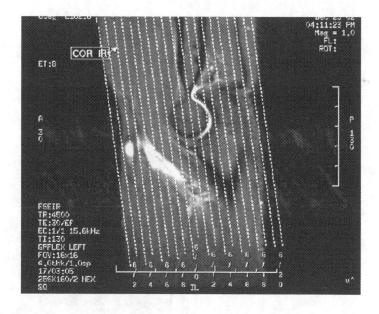

Figure 11-6   **T₁ SAGITTAL IMAGE**

A result of figure 11-1
prescriptioning

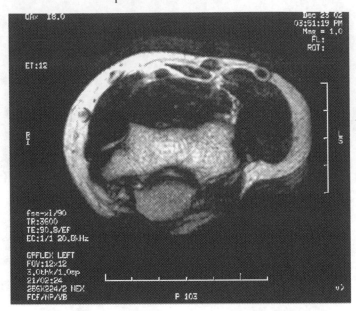

Figure 11-7   **T₁ CORONAL IMAGE**

A result of figure 11-2
prescriptioning

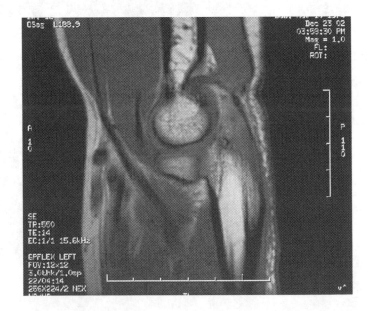

Figure 11-8

CORONAL INVERSION RECOVERY IMAGE

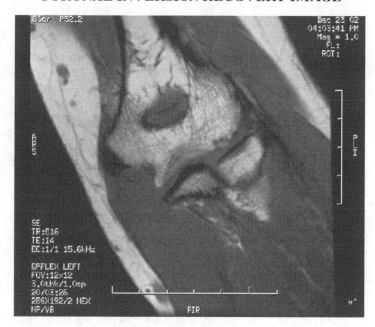

A result of figure 11-4
prescriptioning

Figure 11-9

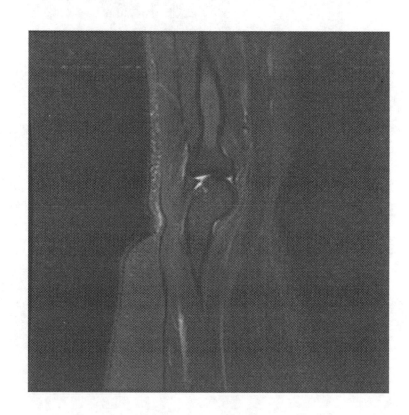

A result of figure 11-3
prescriptioning

Figure 11-10   **SAGITTAL INVERSION RECOVERY IMAGE**

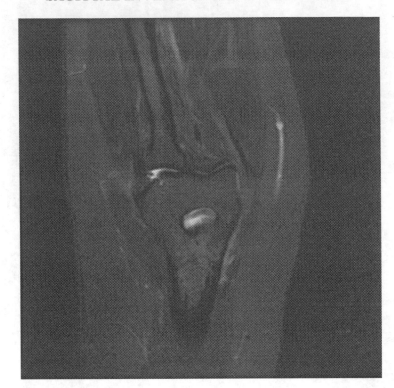

A result of figure 11-3
prescriptioning

CHAPTER 12

SCANNING THE BREAST

INDICATIONS FOR BREAST SCANNING

1. Silicon leak
2. Cancer-Women with breast cancer. BRCA2 [alt.gene]
3. Abnormal mammogram

COIL

The dedicated breast coil is used. This is a phased array, cup shaped coil. This coil provides optimum spatial resolution. Each breast is carefully positioned into each chamber of the coil.

LAND MARKING

The horizontal laser light is crossing the center of both breasts. The longitudinal laser light is passing the midline of the body. It is important to know that there is no compression technique needed to perform MRI of the breast.

POSITIONING

The patient is prone with the feet first. Sponges are placed on the patient's lower legs for comfort. An advantage of this position is that the patient is looking out of the base of the magnet thereby reducing claustrophobia.

SUGGESTED PROTOCOL

1. Vibrant
2. T1 sag Fat SAT SE
3. Stir axial dynamic
4. Sagittal FS axial Stir
5. Axial T_2 FS
6. Axial T_1 No FS

From the 3 pl. localizer, select an axial image and prescribe left to right slices to include the axilla. See image and phasing.

T_1 sagittal image

T_2 sagittal SE-Prescribe the same as above (see figures 12.1 to 12.2).

T_1 sagittal SE FAT SAT
Prescribe the same as above (see figure 12.1)

FIR FS Axials

Select a mid sagittal image. Prescribe superior to inferior. Make sure to apply FAT saturation from the additional parameters. When doing pre scanning it should be done manually.

(See figures 12.5 to 12.8)

Figure 12-1

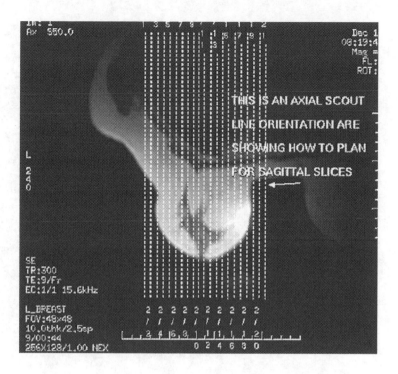

Figure 12-2

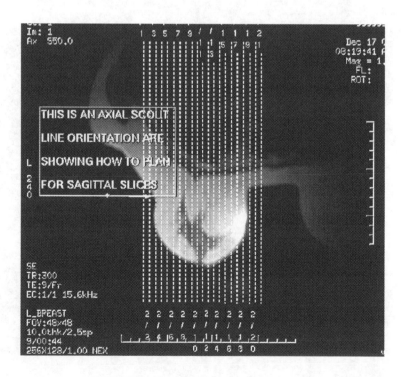

Figure 12-3

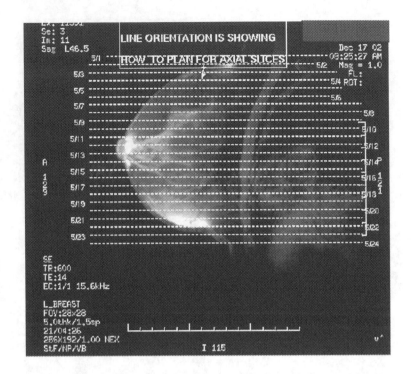

Figure 12-4

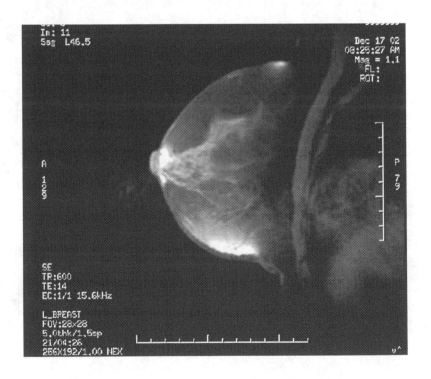

Figure 12-5

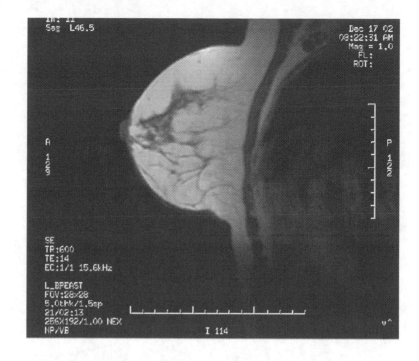

Figure 12-6

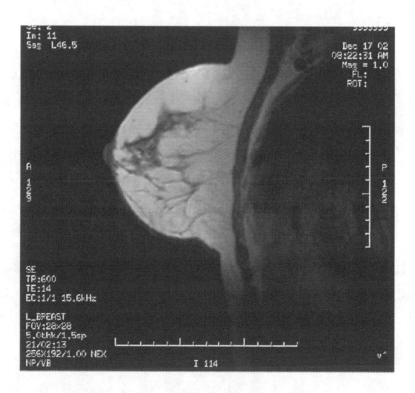

CHAPTER 13

HOW TO SCAN THE CHEST

SOME INDICATIONS FOR SCANNING THE CHEST

1. When patients are contraindicated for CT contrast
2. Neoplasm
3. Aortic aneurysm
4. Aortic Dissection

COIL

The Cardiac coil is commonly used.

All chest examinations must be done with the bellows attached across the chest in order to eliminate motion from respiration.

LAND MARKING

The longitudinal laser light is at the center of the thorax. The horizontal laser light is at the sternal notch.

110

POSITIONING

The patient is lying supine on the table, head first.

SUGGESTED PROTOCOL

A coronal T_1 localizer with a large field of view is performed

1. T_2 Axials FSE
2. T_1 Axials SE
3. Axial Double IR
4. T_1 Sagittal Fiesta
5. T_2 Sagittal GRE
6. T_1 Coronal Fiesta
7. Contrast enhanced MRA FGRE

NOTE: Apply all necessary gating techniques that are available at the particular site.

Saturation pulses should be applied. This method significantly reduces artifacts from flowing blood. If masses are being ruled out, then gadolinium should be administered.

In cases where aortic dilatation is the reason for the examination, then oblique sagittal slices through the aortic arch are prescribed. This prescription must be done on an axial slice that depicts the superior and inferior aorta.

(See figures 13.1 to 13.9)

Figure 13-1   **CORONAL FIESTA**

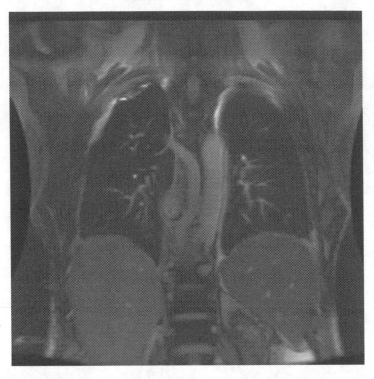

Figure 13-2   **AXIAL FIESTA**

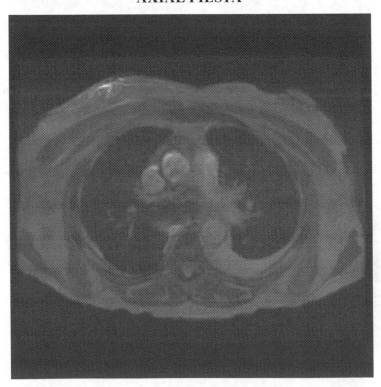

Figure 13-3

AXIAL T²

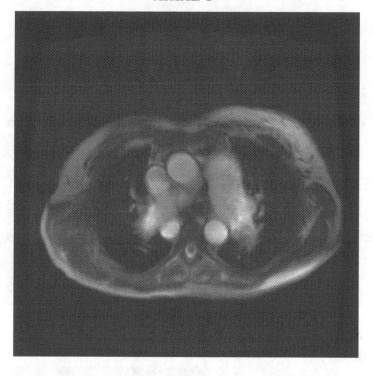

Figure 13-4

AXIAL DOUBLE IR

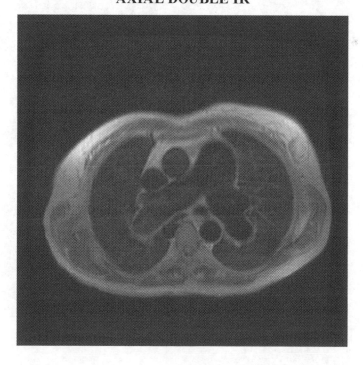

Figure 13-5   **AXIAL T¹**

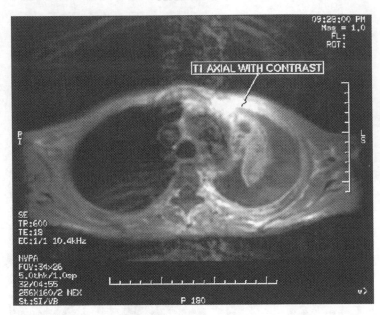

Figure 13-6   **SAGITTAL FIESTA**

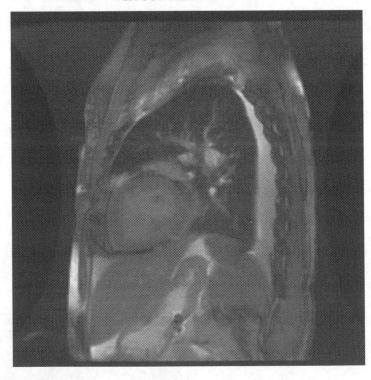

Figure 13-7   **SAGITTAL FIESTA**

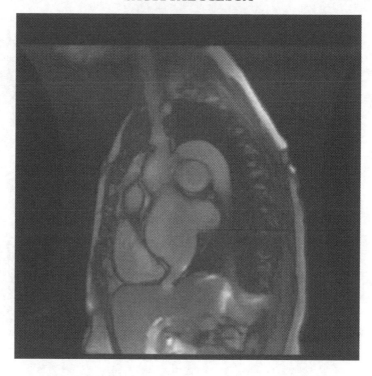

Figure 13-8   **SAGITTAL GRE**

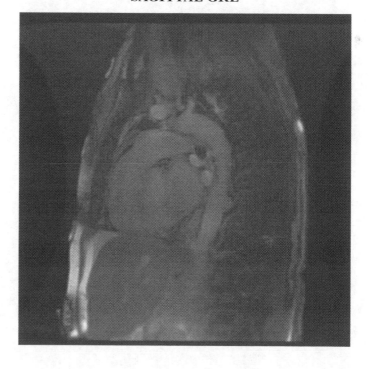

Figure 13-9   **CE MRA FGRE**

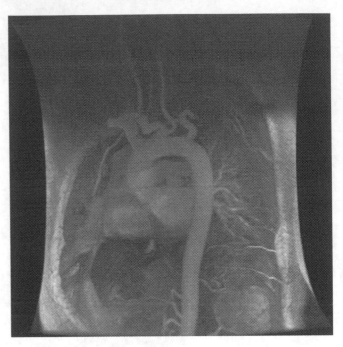

CHAPTER 14

HOW TO SCAN THE HEART

POSITIONING

Patient is supine, feet first with the cardiac coil carefully attached. Top and bottom must match. Vector gating is a must. The patient must be shaved before placing the EKG quad nodes. Proper placement is very important and the patient must practice breathing instructions before scanning.

Landmark-At the center of the coil.

A coronal scout is obtained

SOME INDICATIONS FOR SCANNING THE HEART

1. Pericarditis-This is an inflammation around the sac containing the heart

2. Coronary artery disease-The build up of plaque inside the coronary arteries, the vessels that supply oxygenated blood to the heart muscles.
3. Congestive heart disease-Defects of the structures of the heart (e.g. septal defect of the ventricles).
4. Aneurism-Dilatation of part of the heart vessels such as the aorta
5. Valve abnormality-Abnormal functioning of the heart.

WITH THE ABOVE INDICATIONS A CARDIAC MRI/MRA IS PERFORMED

Cardiac imaging is performed to obtain images of the heart and arteries non-invasively. The images are obtained from both stationary tissue and moving structures of the heart.

Specific protocols are used depending on the history of the patient. Protocols dictates how the images will look. Prescriptioning is therefore very important.

TECHNIQUES:

1. Fiesta (Fast Image Employing Steady State Acquisition)
2. SSFPR (Steady State Free Precession)
3. FISP (Fast Imaging with Steady State Precession)
4. FFE (Fast Field Echo)
5. IR (Inversion Recovery).

PLANES

1. Coronary localizer
2. Sagittal Cine (candy cane)
3. Coronal Cine (3 Cannel)
4. Right ventricle, Long axis, PA outflow, Coronal Dynamic

5. Aorta TSE, AX Dark Blood
6. Axial 3 Chamber FFSPR (FISP)- Bright Blood
7. Coronal Cine
8. Aortic Valve
9. Test Bolus
10. Sagittal Aorta
11. Axial T1 post

THE SUGGESTED PROTOCOL FOR THE ISCHEMIC HEART:

1. Sagittal Localizer
2. Fiesta Axial
3. Mitral valve long axis 2 chamber. 2D Fiesta
4. 4 channel 2D Fiesta
5. Short axis Cine-Use asset to reduce scan time.
6. FGRET 4 channel
7. Radial short axis IR-Double IR and triple IR

Figure 14-1

2 chamber scanning is done for both the right side and the left side of the heart.

<u>Right side-2 chamber scanning will demonstrate:</u>

a-Aortic root

b-Right atrium

c-Tricuspid valve

<u>Left side- 2 chamber will demonstrate:</u>

a-Left ventricle

b-Left atrium

c-Mitral valve

3D TOF MRA OF AORTA

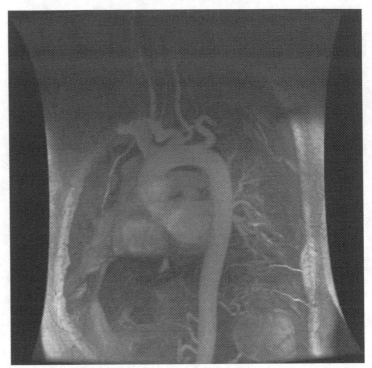

Figure 14-2

AXIAL TWO CHAMBER

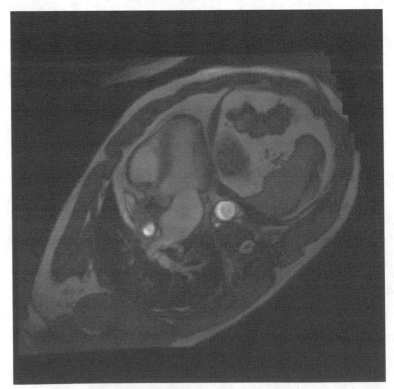

2 chamber scanning will demonstrate:

a-Aortic root

b-Left ventricle

c-Mitral valve

Figure 14-3

2D FIESTA

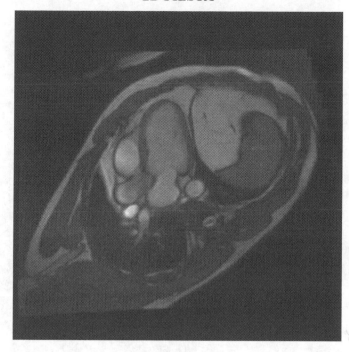

4 chamber scanning will
demonstrate:
a-Interventricular
septum
b-Tricuspid valve
c-Mitral valve

Figure 14-4

CORONAL SCOUT

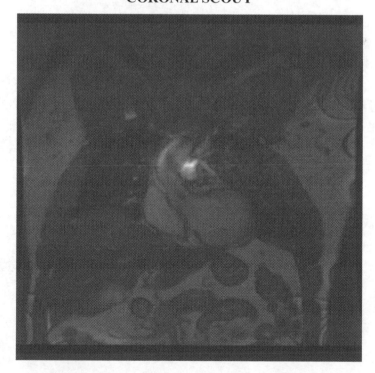

LVOT-Left ventricular
outflow track, aortic
valve, ascending Aorta

121

Figure 14-5

TWO CHAMBER FIESTA

Double IRGRE-Will
demonstrate black
blood. Done with
Gadolinium mainly to
differentiate between
flowing blood and a
cardiac mass. This is the
viability sequence that
differentiates infarction
from myocardium.
Note that black blood
imaging can be obtained
using a spin echo
sequence with high TE
and thin slices.
Images will demonstrate
the heart muscles being
dark while an infarct
will appear bright

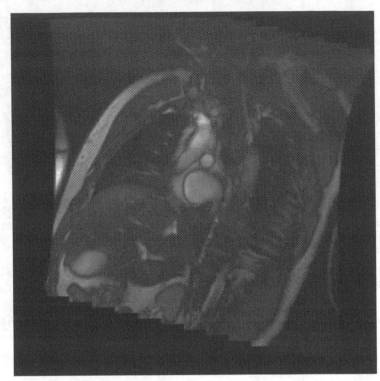

Figure 14-6

FOUR CHAMBER FIESTA

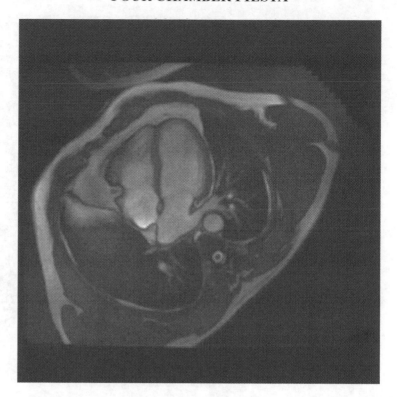

Cine- Demonstrates the heart beat in frames per second. Cine uses ECG vector gating to measure the heart rate. The pulse sequences of choice are SSFPR, FTE or FISP. The slice thickness must be very thin and the interleave scanning method must be used

Figure 14-7

AXIAL FIESTA

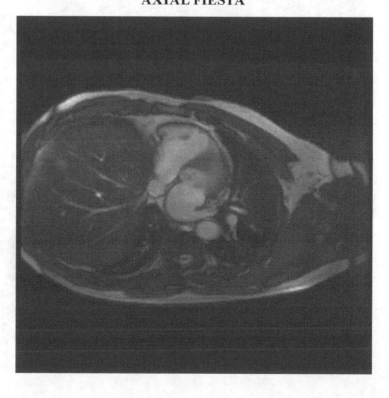

Figure 14-8   **FOUR CHAMBER AXIAL FIESTA**

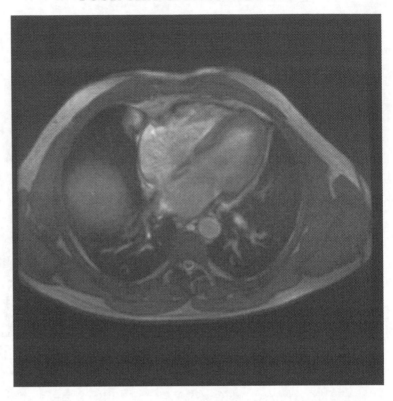

Figure 14-9   **AXIAL CINE**

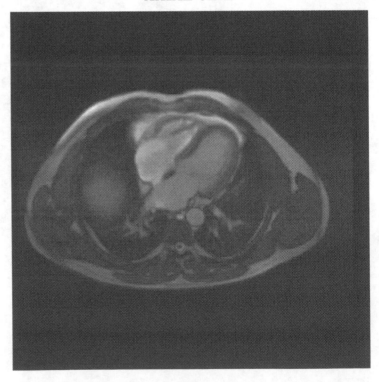

Figure 14-10   **TWO CHAMBER CORONAL**

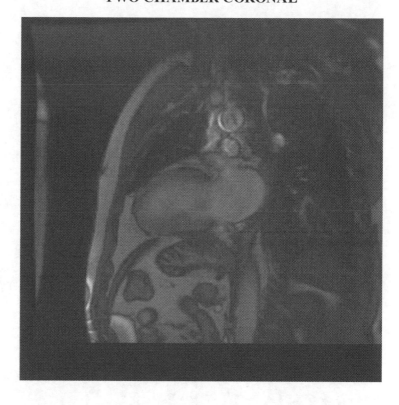

Figure 14-11   **DOUBLE INVERSION RECOVERY SAGITTAL**

CHAPTER 15

HOW TO SCAN THE BRACHIAL PLEXUS

SOME INDICATIONS FOR SCANNING THE BRACHIAL PLEXUS

1. Lesions
2. Trauma

COIL

The body coil or the c-spine coil should be used

Attaching the bellows will be helpful for this study

LAND MARKING

The longitudinal laser light is at the center of the thorax. The horizontal laser light is at the sternal notch.

POSITIONING

The patient is lying supine on the table, head first.

SUGGESTED PROTOCOL

A coronal localizer with a large field of view to illustrate both armpit areas is performed. In order to eliminate flow void artifacts from the Carotid Arteries and the Jugular Veins, SAT pulses should be placed in both the superior and inferior aspect of the arteries and veins when prescribing the actual sequences.

PRE-CONTRAST THIN SLICES	POST CONTRAST
1. T_2 Axials FSE	1. T_1 Axials SE
2. T_1 Axials SE	2. T_1 Coronal SE
3. T_1 Coronal SE	
4. T_2 Axials FAT SAT	

(See figures 15.1 to 15.8)

Figure 15-1

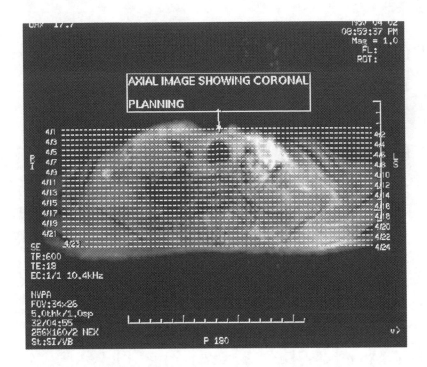

Figure 15-2

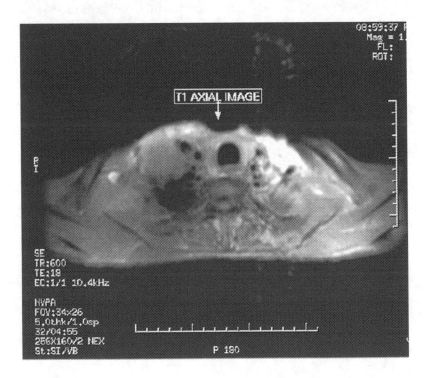

Figure 15-3

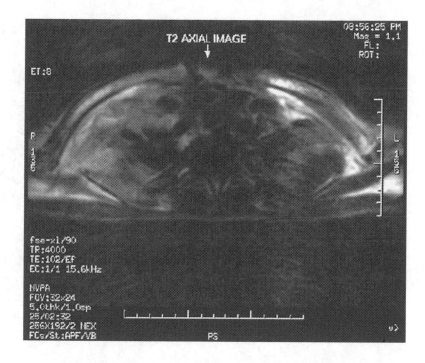

Figure 15-4

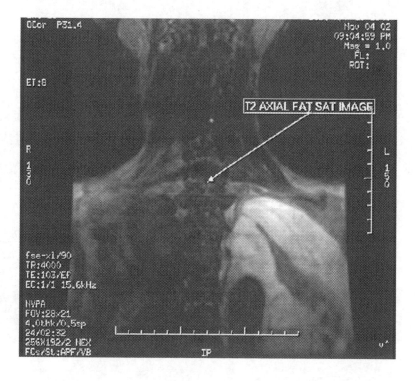

Figure 15-5

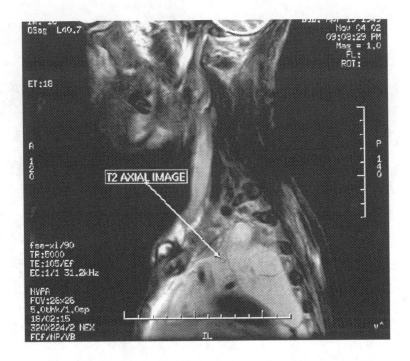

Figure 15-6

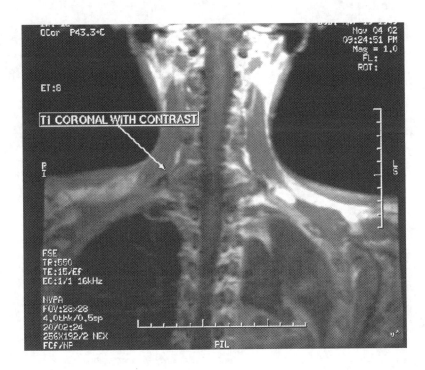

CHAPTER 16

HOW TO SCAN THE ABDOMEN

SOME INDICATIONS FOR SCANNING THE ABDOMEN

1. Liver lesions
2. Hemangiomas
3. Metastatic Disease
4. Pancreatic diseases
5. Kidney Cysts/lesions

COIL

The body coil, the torso phased array coil or the cardiac coilis used and the bellows is connected across the lower chest area.

LAND MARKING

The longitudinal laser light is at the midline of the body. The horizontal laser light passes through then xiphoid.

POSITIONING

The patient is lying supine on the table, feet first, hands above the head is preferred to eliminate artifacts

SUGGESTED PROTOCOL

The protocol varies depending on the site. A coronal localizer is accomplished. Axial slices will cover from the superior aspect of the dome of the liver to the iliac crest.

STANDARD ABDOMEN PROTOCOL WO/W CONTRAST EXCEPT LIVER STUDIES

1. In/out phase T_1 GRE
2. Coronal T_2 SSFSE
3. Axial T_1 Lava
4. Coronal T_1 Lava
5. Axial T_2 SSFSE
6. Axial T_2 FSE Far Sat
7. Post contrast
8. Coronal T_1 GRE
9. Axial T_1, Sagittal T_1, Coronal T_1
   a. Dynamic scanning should be done with contrast if looking for liver lesions.
   b. Thin sections are done through the kidneys if focus is on the kidneys.
   c. MRA of the renal arteries is done to rule out renal artery stenosis. In addition to the above pulse sequences, a 3D coronal contrast enhanced MRA is performed.

On an Axial image, the aorta (at about T6) is located and a "tracker" is placed over it. Then an Axial slice showing both kidneys is used to prescribe the 3D coronal. The SAT pulse is placed inferiorly to avoid venous flow contamination

NOTE: The utilization of a power injector will allow you to set; A timed pressure rate (per second)
    d. A volume
    e. An injection delay if necessary is best for this study.

Upon reconstruction of the maximum intensity projection image, rotation should to the right for one series and inferiorly for a second set of series. These will best demonstrate the arteries.

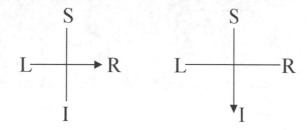

THIS IS AN AXIAL IMAGE WHICH IS A RESULT OF THE ABOVE PRESCRIBED LINES

Figure 16-1

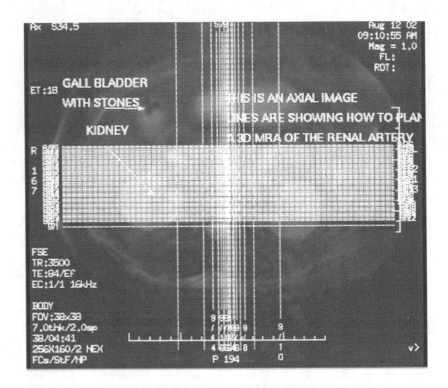

Figure 16-2

A result of figure 16-1
prescriptioning

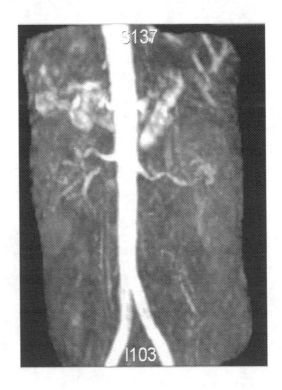

Figure 16-3

CORONAL SCOUT SHOWING AXIAL PLANNING

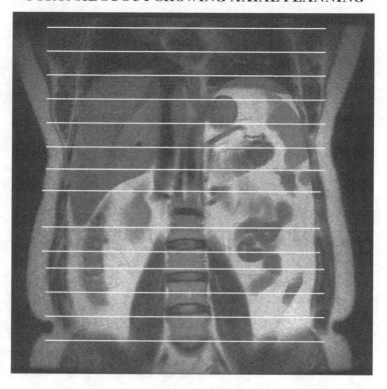

Figure 16-4

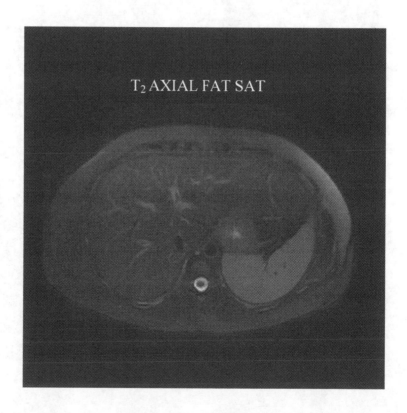

T₂ AXIAL FAT SAT

Figure 16-5

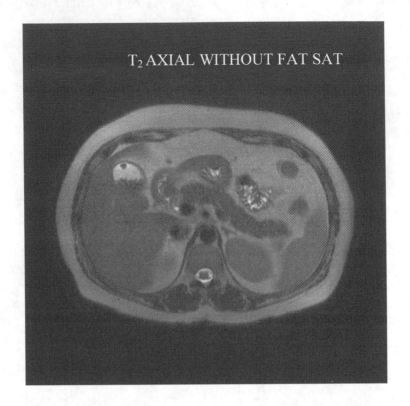

T₂ AXIAL WITHOUT FAT SAT

Figure 16-6

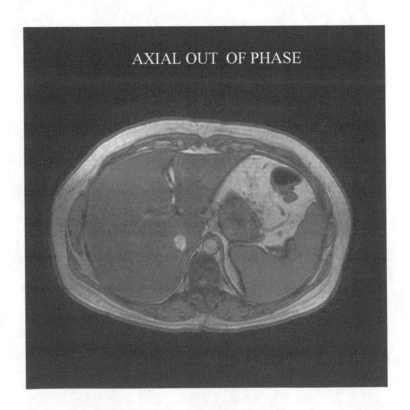

AXIAL OUT OF PHASE

Figure 16-7

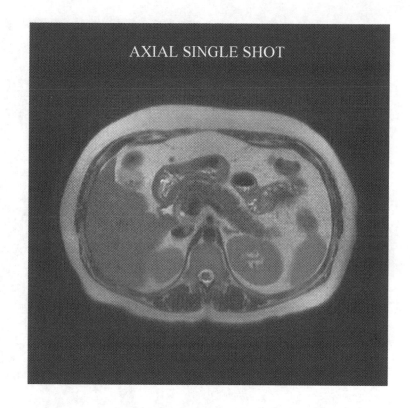

Figure 16-8

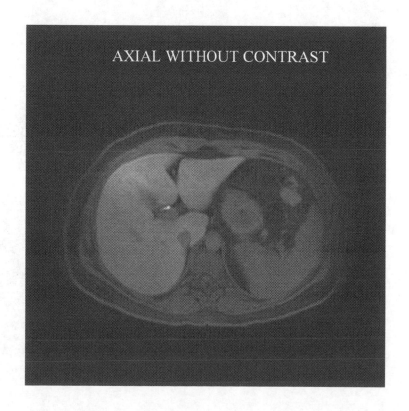

Figure 16-9

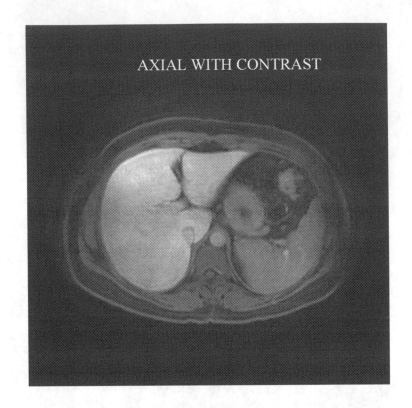

AXIAL WITH CONTRAST

Figure 16-10

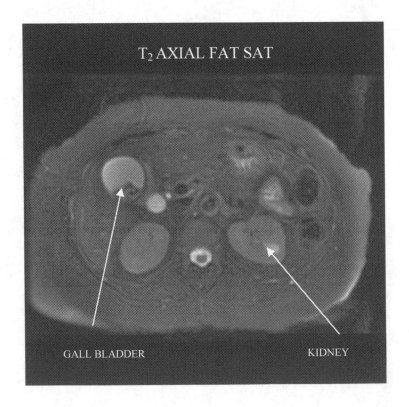

T₂ AXIAL FAT SAT

GALL BLADDER   KIDNEY

Figure 16-11

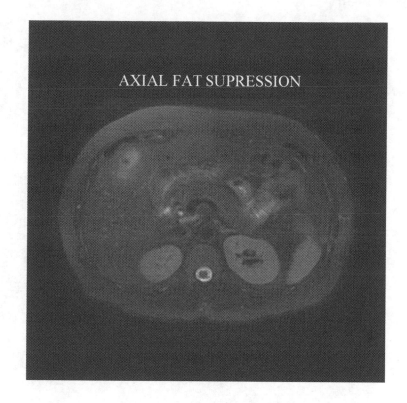

Figure 16-12

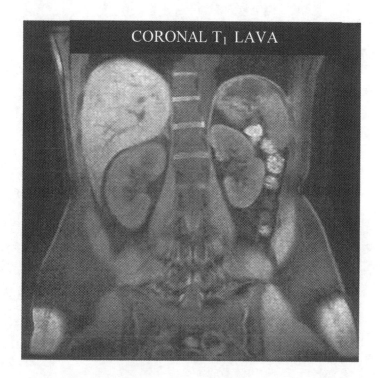

Figure 16-13

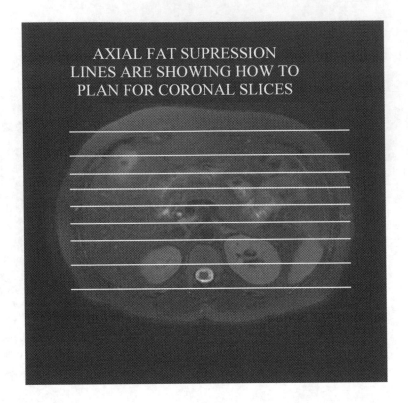

CHAPTER 17

MRCP

SOME INDICATIONS FOR MRCP STUDIES

1. Common Bile Duct dilatation
2. Failed Endoscopic Retrograde CholangioPancreatogrophy (ERCP)
3. Gallbladder functioning

COIL

The phased array torso coil is used.

LAND MARKING

The horizontal laser light is crossing the xiphoid. The longitudinal laser light is passing the midline of the body.

POSITIONING

The patient is supine with the feet first. The bellows is attached. This will be very beneficial when applying the breath hold technique. Particular attention must be given to proper positioning making sure that the patient is located on the magnetic component of the table. Every table has a point that a patient must be situated below the point otherwise positioning may fail or loss of signal will occur.

Instruct the patient that when told not to breath they should stop breathing.

SUGGESTED PROTOCOL

A coronal localizer image is performed. This image will demonstrate the Gallbladder, its ducts in relation to the Pancreas and its ducts.

The patient must be NPO

THE TECHNIQUE FOR THE LOCALIZER IS:

- Minimum TR
- Minimum TE
- Bandwidth of 62.5
- SS FSE
- 256 x 128 Matrix
- FOV 40
- Thickness 7 x 2, 9 slices

MRCP thick slab-axial and coronal
MRCP thin slice-axial and coronal

1. Localizer
2. Coronal T_2 FSE

3. 3D/2D MRCP post contrast Axial, Coronal Lava
4. In/out phase
5. Axial T_1 Lava
6. Coronal T_1 Lava
7. Axial T_2 FSE
8. Axial T_2 FSE FS

MRCP THICK SLAB AXIAL

From the coronal localizer, prescribe the slab over the gallbladder. Make sure to start superiorly enough to include the entire biliary tree in relation to the pancreas. More than one slab can be used. After prescription is done, do "breadth hold" technique. Instruct the patient to hold suspend respiration and start scanning. This should only take 2-8 seconds.

MRCP THIN SLICE AXIALS

This is done exactly as above except that the prescription is now done on an axial slice that demonstrates the gallbladder.

MRCP THIN SLICE AXIALS/CORONALS
and MRCP THIN SLICE AXIALS

From the coronal scout prescribe over the gallbladder. Use the same method as above.

MRCP THIN SLICE CORONAL

From an axial slice showing the gallbladder, prescribe slices to cover the gallbladder in its entirety.

(See figure 17.1)

Figure 17-1

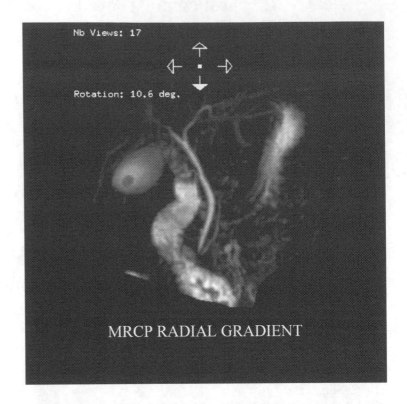

MRCP RADIAL GRADIENT

Figure 17-2

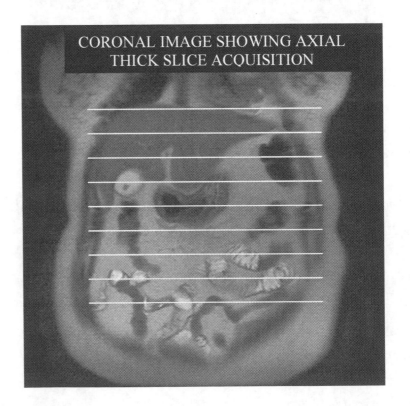

CORONAL IMAGE SHOWING AXIAL
THICK SLICE ACQUISITION

Figure 17-3

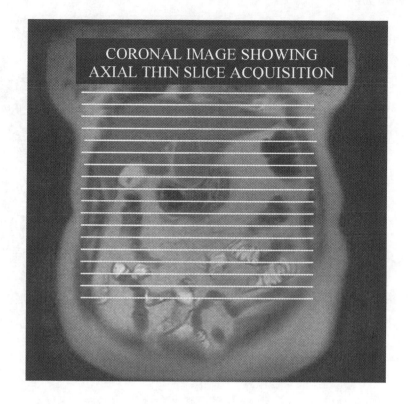

Figure 17-4

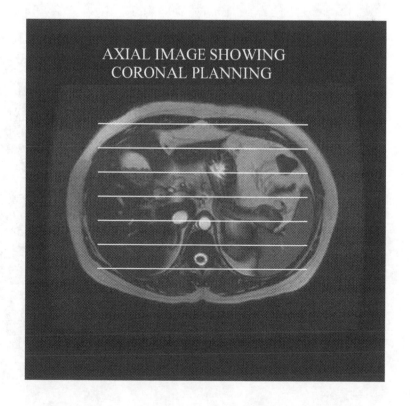

Figure 17-5

A result of figure 17-4
prescriptioning

CORONAL THICK SLICE

Figure 17-5

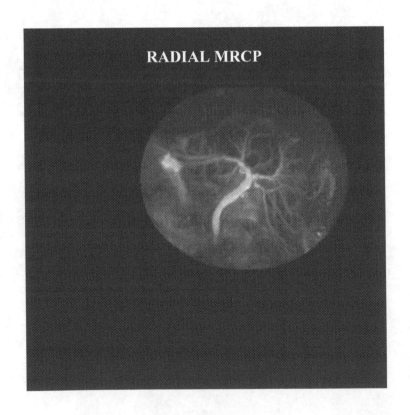

RADIAL MRCP

CHAPTER 18

MRV OF THE ABDOMEN

INDICATIONS FOR MRV OF THE ABDOMEN

1. Extremity swelling
2. Vena Cava thrombosis

The MRV of the Abdomen is performed with and without contrast.

COIL

The body coil or the torso coil is used

LANDMARKING

The horizontal laser light is at the xiphoid. The longitudinal laser light is at the midline of the body

POSITIONING

Patient is supine, feet first

SUGGESTED PROTOCOL

2-D TOF SPGR is prescribed axially on a coronal image, the following should be performed to maximize the quality of the scan:

1. From the saturation menu, activate the CONCAT SAT technique
2. Saturation band must be placed superior. Use a thickness of about 80.
3. On the vascular screen, the "collapse" must be on and select 1g on the projection image.

3-D TOF/F SPGR with contrast is done coronally on an axial image using "smart prep". The same as described under renal artery examination except that MRV is performed in multiphase and a delay of about six seconds is set after injection.

(See figures 18.1 to 18.16)

Figure 18-1

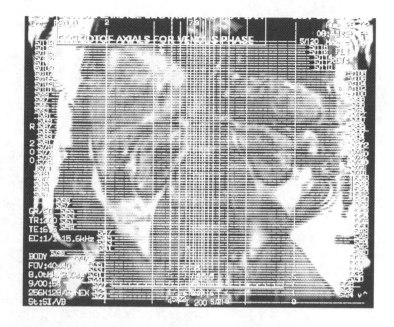

Figure 18-2

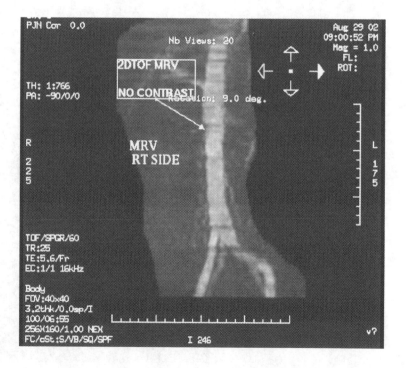

Figure 18-3

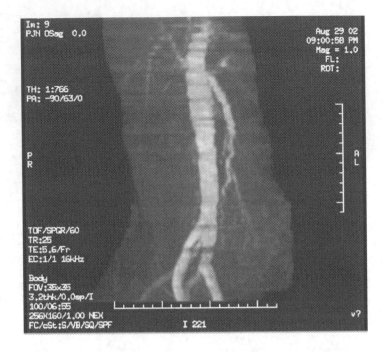

Figure 18-4

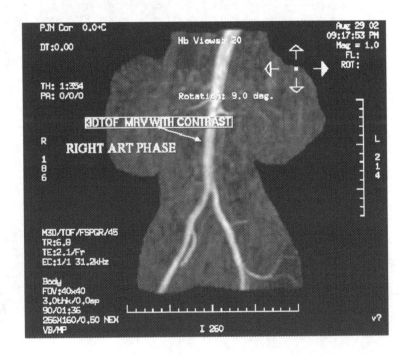

Figure 18-5

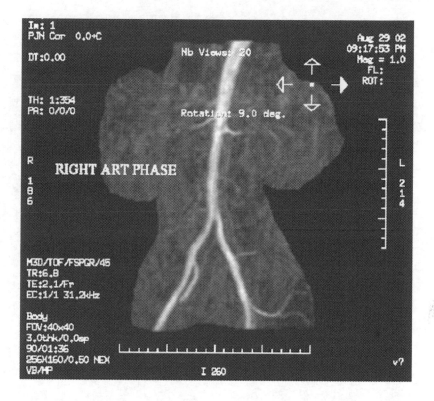

Figure 18-6

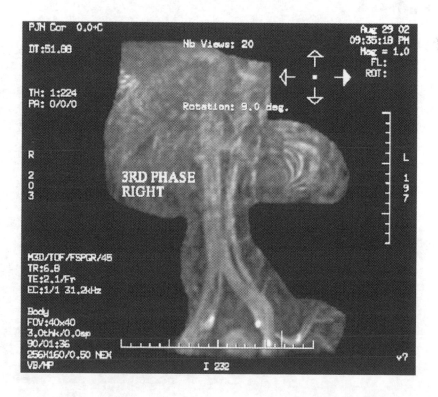

Figure 18-7

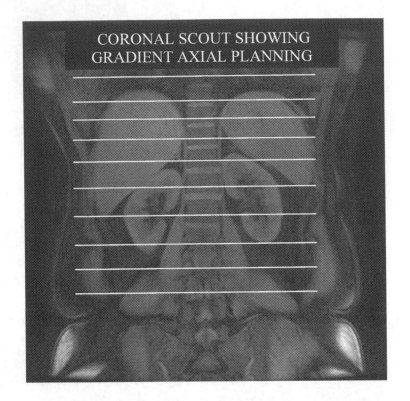

Figure 18-8

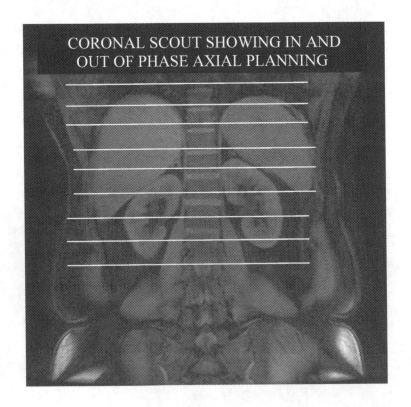

Figure 18-9

A result of figure 18-7
prescriptioning

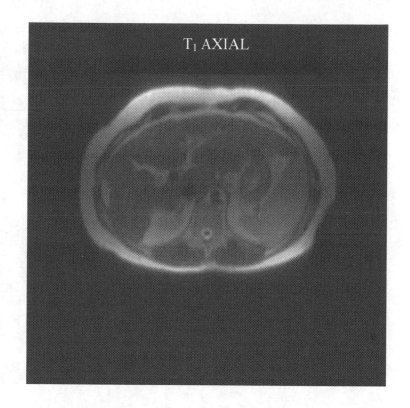

Figure 18-10

A result of figure 18-8
prescriptioning

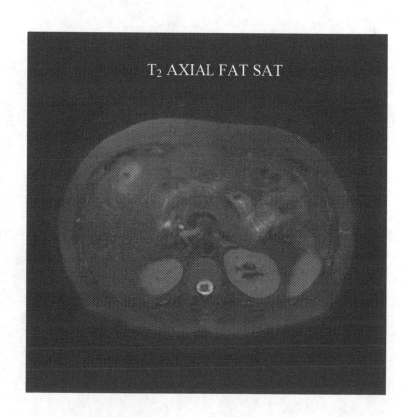

Figure 18-11

Out of phase:
The TE selected is half
of the in phase. For
example TE for out of
phase is 2. TE for in
phase would be 4

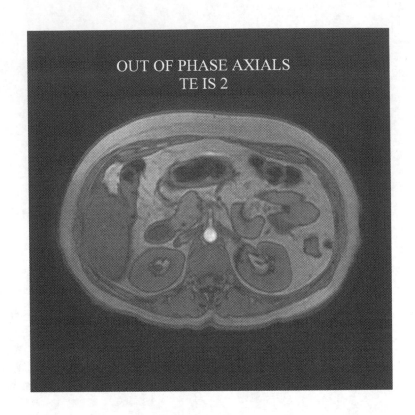

Figure 18-12

In phase-TE 4

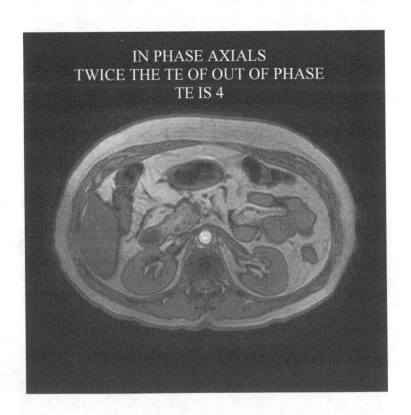

Figure 18-13

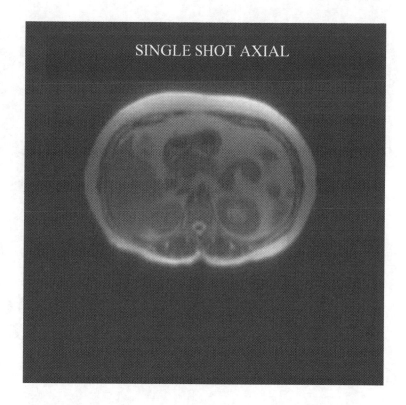

SINGLE SHOT AXIAL

Figure 18-14

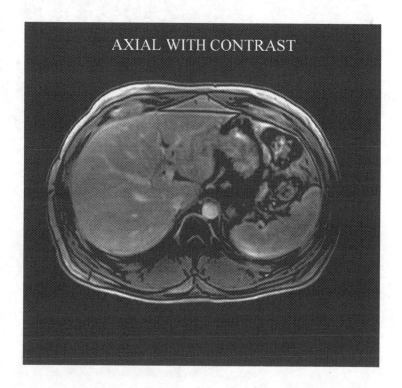

AXIAL WITH CONTRAST

Figure 18-15

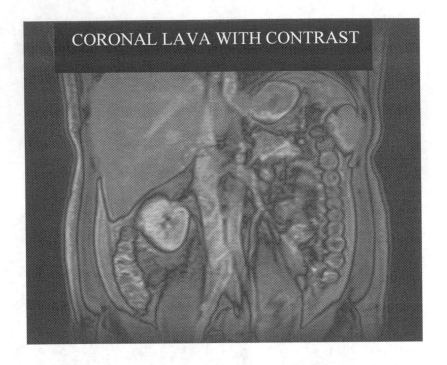

Figure 18-16

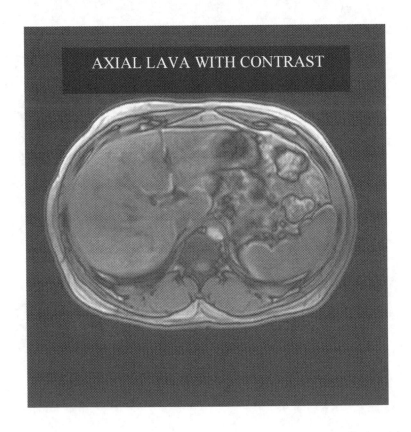

CHAPTER 19

HOW TO SCAN THE RENAL ARTERY

SOME INDICATIONS FOR SCANNING THE RENAL ARTERY

1. Hypertension
2. Diabetes Mellitus

COIL

The phased array torso coil is selected and care should be taken for proper connection and placement

LAND MARKING

The longitudinal laser light is at the midline of the body. The horizontal laser light is crossing the xiphoid.

POSITIONING

The patient is supine with the feet going in first. The body is very straight. The Bellows is attached around the upper abdomen. This will eliminate breathing motion. It will also show on the control monitor on the console the way the patient is breathing thus enabling the use of the breath-hold technique. Instruct the patient to listen for breathing instructions.

SUGGESTED PROTOCOL

The power injector is loaded with gadolinium in Syringe A. Syringe B is loaded with 30 ml of bacteriostatic sodium chloride .9%. Depending on the sites, the amount of gadolinium used varies but 30 ml is commonly used.

An Angiocath is placed in the antecubital vein securely taped down with an opsite. The angiocath is then attached to the power injector.

A pressure rate of between 1.5 cc to 2.5 cc per second is set from the control monitor.

The protocol applied depends and varies on the site of interest. However, the following are suggested.

1. A coronal localizer
2. Axial locator slices
3. Axial T_2 FSE
4. 3D coronal smart prep
5. T_1 axial post

TECHNIQUE

From the coronal localizer, prescribe about six slices at the area of T 12. From these slices, the one that best depicts the aorta will be used for the "Tracking Device".

From the coronal localizer, also prescribe the T_2 axials from the dome of the liver to the iliac crest.

3D CORONAL SMART PREP

From the T_2 axial sequence, select the slice that demonstrates the kidneys in full profile. The prescribed lines are placed in such a way so that the superior aspect of the kidneys to the inferior aspect of the kidneys are covered completely. Pick an axial image from the axial localizer that shows the aorta. On the image, the tracker is placed right on the aorta. Aorta

Tracker

The length and the width of the tracker is adjusted to coincide with the circumference of the artery.

Prescribe the 3D coronal On the T_2 axial slice that demonstrates the kidneys. This is on thick slab. The slab is placed to cover the kidneys starting a little above the kidneys. On the scan monitor, make sure to type in the amount of gadolinium and the type of gadolinium in the required fields. At this point, the injector is armed making sure that all air is expelled from the syringe and the tubing.

From the pre-scan menu, perform "Prep Scan" then press "Start Scan". Be very alert to the messages on the message center. The monitor will first say "acquiring baseline" then that will change to "Begin Injection".

Immediately instruct the patient to hold his or her breath. Press the "Start Injection" button located on the power injector control monitor. "Bolus Detected" will appear on the message center if the injection is successful.

(See figures 19.1 to 19.7)

Figure 19-1   **THIS IS A CORONAL 3D MRA IMAGE DEMONSTRATING THE AORTA AND THE RENAL ARTERIES WHICH IS A RESULT OF THE PRESCRIBED LINES BOLUS PHASE**

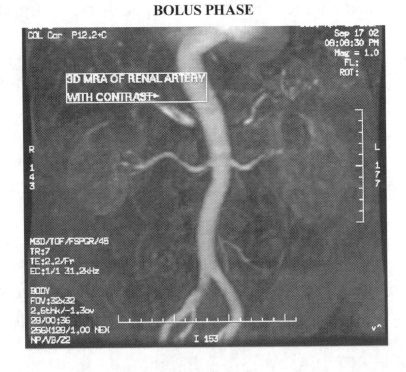

Figure 19-2   **THIS IS THE FIRST PHASE OF CONTRAST UTILIZING**

A SMART PREP MODE OF INJECTION

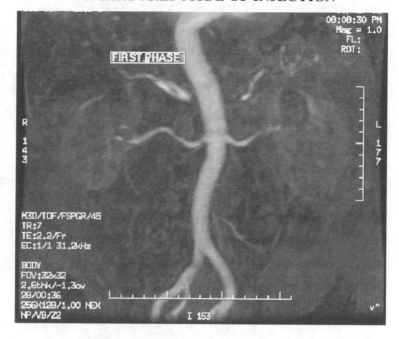

Figure 19-3   **THIS IS THE SECOND PHASE (NON EQUILIBRIUM)**

DEMONSTRATING THE CONTRAST LEAVING THE AORTA

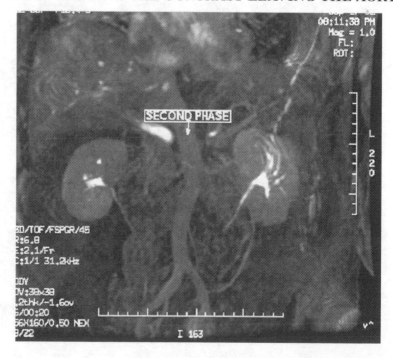

Figure 19-4   **THIS IS THE THIRD AND FINAL PHASE (EQUILIBRIUM) DEMONSTRATING THE CONTRAST LEAVING THE RENAL ARTERY**

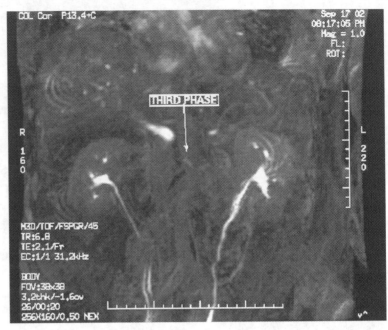

Figure 19-5

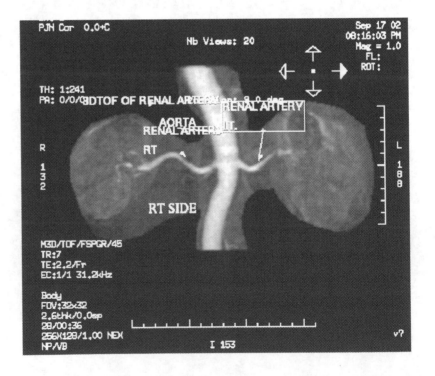

Figure 19-6

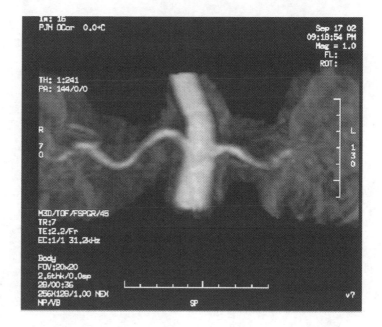

CHAPTER 20

HOW TO SCAN THE FEMALE PELVIS

SOME INDICATIONS FOR SCANNING THE FEMALE PELVIS

1. Cancer of the uterus
2. Fibroids
3. Placenta accreta/ Previa
4. Breech
5. All forms of pelvic disorders

COIL

Torso Phased Array

LAND MARKING

The longitudinal laser light is at the midline of the pelvis. The horizontal laser light is crossing about 2 inches below the iliac crest.

POSITIONING

The patient is supine with the feet first.

SUGGESTED PROTOCOL

The protocol applied depends and varies on the site of interest. However, the following are suggested.

1. A coronal fast spin echo is performed as a localizer
2. Axial T_1 SE
3. Axial T_2 FSE
4. SS FSE axials
5. Sagittal T_2 FSE
6. Sagittal T_2 FSE FAT SAT
7. Coronal T_2 FSE FAT SAT

AXIAL T_2 FSE

Select a mid coronal slice from the localizer series and prescribe axial slices from the top of the iliac crest to the inferior aspect of the symphysis pubis.

T_1 AXIALS

Select a mid coronal slice from the localizer series and prescribe axial slices from the top of the iliac crest to the inferior aspect of the symphysis pubis.

SS FSE AXIALS

Select a mid coronal slice from the localizer series and prescribe axial slices from the top of the iliac crest to the inferior aspect of the symphysis pubis.

T_2 SAGITTAL

Select a mid coronal slice and prescribe the sagittal slices from left to right to include the acetabulum on both sides and the iliac crest to the symphysis pubis from the top to the bottom.

T_2 SAGITTAL FS

Select a mid coronal slice and prescribe the sagittal slices from left to right to include the acetabulum on both sides and the iliac crest to the symphysis pubis from the top to the bottom.

T_2 CORONAL

Select a mid axial slice and prescribe the lines from anterior to posterior on the image. This will result in anterior to posterior slicing in the coronal plane.

(See figures 20-1 to 20-9)

NOTE: Use the smallest FOV possible. When doing this, apply the "no phase wrap" on the imaging options menu. This will eliminate the wraparound artifact. See example of wraparound artifact figure 20.9

SCANNING THE FEMALE PELVIS

Figure 20-1

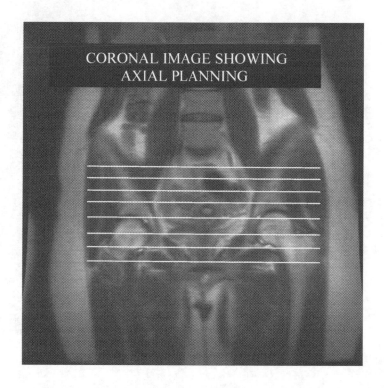

CORONAL IMAGE SHOWING
AXIAL PLANNING

Figure 20-2

CORONAL IMAGE SHOWING
SAGITTAL PLANNING

167

Figure 20-3

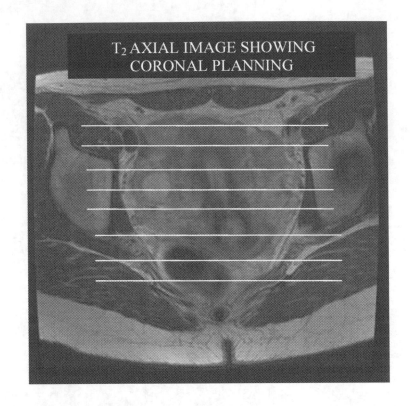

Figure 20-4

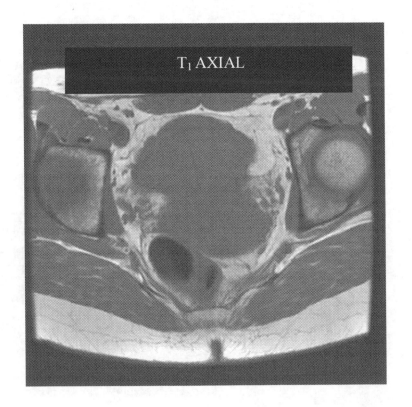

Figure 20-5

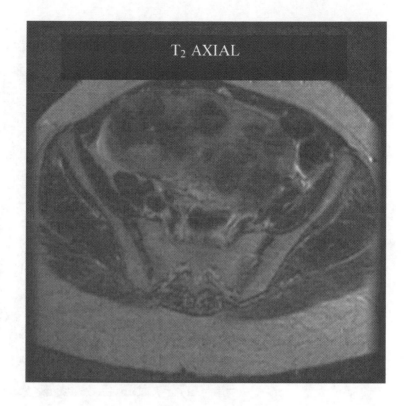

T₂ AXIAL

Figure 20-6

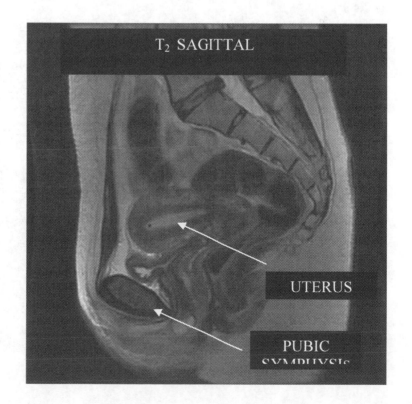

T₂ SAGITTAL

UTERUS

PUBIC
SYMPHYSIS

Figure 20-7

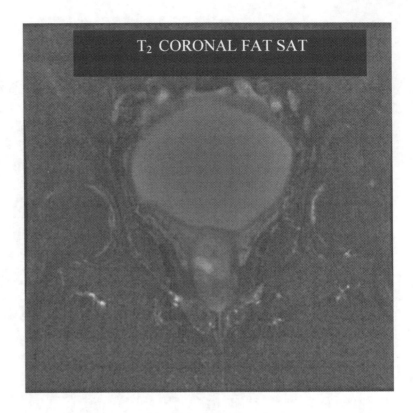

Figure 20-8

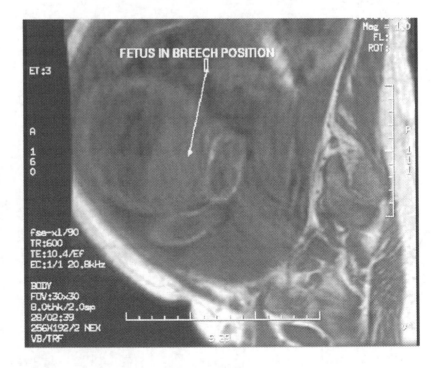

Figure 20-9

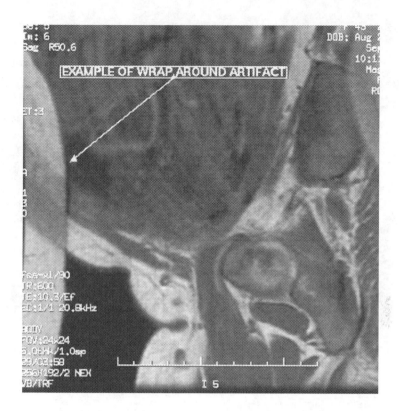

CHAPTER 21

HOW TO SCAN THE PELVIS/HIPS

SOME INDICATIONS FOR SCANNING THE PELVIS/HIPS

1. Avascular Necrosis
2. Fluid effusions
3. Osteomyelitis

POSITIONING

The patient is supine with the feet first.

COIL

Torso Phase Array coil is used

LAND MARKING

The longitudinal laser light is at the midline of the pelvis. The horizontal laser light is crossing about 2 inches below the iliac crest.

SUGGESTED PROTOCOL

1. A coronal localizer is performed
2. Axial T_1 SE
3. Axial T_2 FSE
4. Coronal T_1 SE
5. Coronal STIR
6. Sagittal T_1 SE

AXIAL T_1 SE

Select a mid coronal image and prescribe from above the acetabulum to the proximal femur below.

AXIAL T_2 FSE

Select a mid coronal imager and prescribe from above the acetabulum to the proximal femur below.

CORONAL T_1 SE

Select an axial image demonstrating the femoral heads. Both sides are to be in full profile. Prescribe lines from anterior to the posterior to include the entire femoral joint space.

CORONAL STIR

Select an axial image demonstrating the femoral heads. Both sides are to be in full profile. Prescribe lines from anterior to the posterior to include the entire femoral joint space.

SAGITTAL T₁

Select an axial slice that demonstrates the femoral head. Each slice is performed separately. Prescribe lines from the left to the right to cover the entire acetabulum.

NOTE: Use the smallest FOV possible. When doing this, apply the "no phase wrap" on the imaging options menu. This will eliminate the wraparound artifact. See example of wraparound artifact.

(See figures 21.1 to 21.5)

HOW TO SCAN A PELVIS/HIPS

Figure 21-1

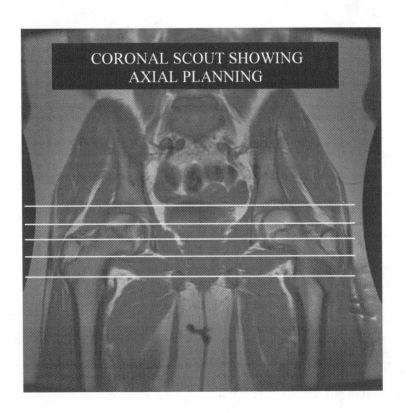

CORONAL SCOUT SHOWING AXIAL PLANNING

Figure 21-2   **HOW TO PLAN SAGITTALS FROM AN AXIAL IMAGE**

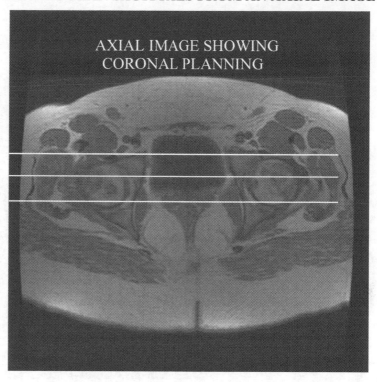

Figure 21-3

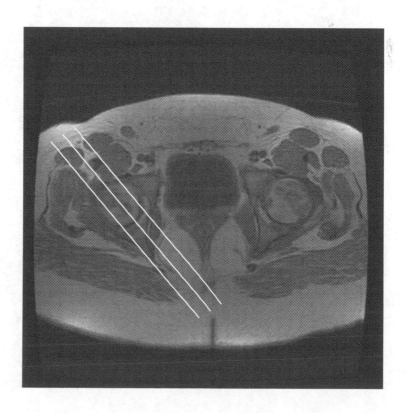

Figure 21-4   **CORONAL IMAGE SHOWING RIGHT SAGITTAL PLANNING**

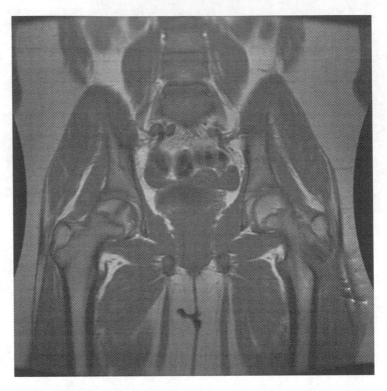

Figure 21-5   **CORONAL IMAGE SHOWING LEFT SAGITTAL PLANNING**

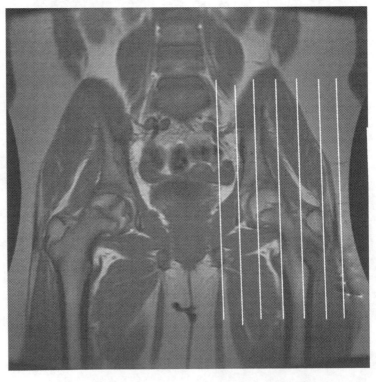

Figure 21-6

T₁ AXIAL IMAGE

T2 AXIAL FAT SAT

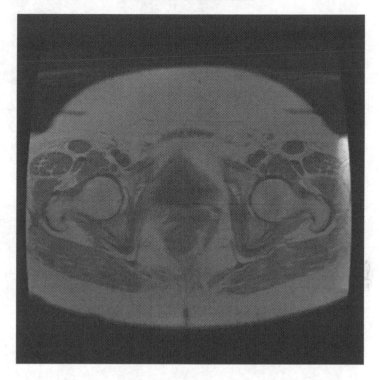

Figure 21-7

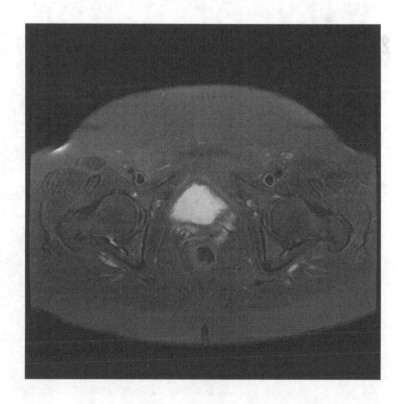

Figure 21-8   **T₁ CORONAL FAT SAT**

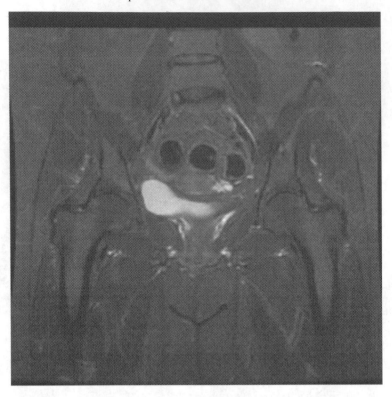

Figure 21-9   **T₁ CORONAL GRE**

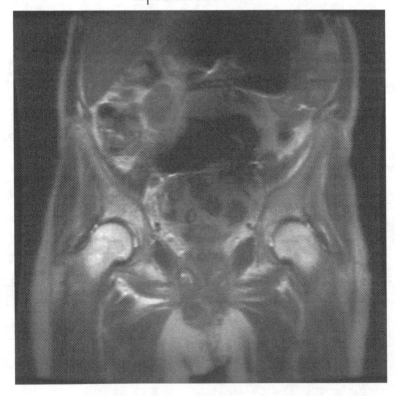

Figure 21-10

SAGITTAL T$_2$

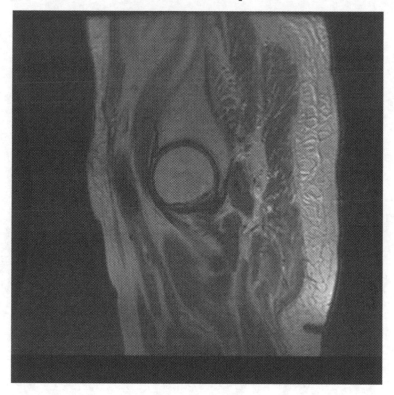

CHAPTER 22

HOW TO SCAN AN MRA OF THE LOWER EXTREMITY

SOME INDICATIONS FOR SCANNING AN MRA OF THE LOWER EXTREMITIES

1. Non healing ulcer
2. Gangrene of the toes
3. Blockage of collateral flow

POSITIONING

The patient is supine with the feet first.

COIL

The wraparound peripheral vascular coil is used if available at the site. If not, then a combination of the head coil and the body coil can be used.

LAND MARKING

With the head coil attached, the feet are positioned securely with sponges on both sides. The longitudinal laser light is at the midline whereas the horizontal laser light is crossing the base of the metatarsals.

SUGGESTED PROTOCOL

A localizer of both feet is performed in the coronal plane. Select a mid coronal image and prescribe the 2D TOF axials to entirely cover both feet (see figure 21.1). At this point the head coil is detached and taken out. The body coil is now used. A new landmark is set at the mid Tibia/Fibula area. a 3-plane T_2^* coronal localizer is again obtained.

Select a mid coronal image displaying both legs. Prescribe the 2D TOF axials to cover both legs. A FOV of 46 is desirable in order to cover slightly above the knees. (See figure 22.8).

A new landmark is again selected. The area of the Femur is now scanned. Prescribe the 2D TOF to include an overlap of the knee to the proximal Femur (46 FOV) (See figure 21.7). A new landmark is again selected. This time it is set at the pelvic area. Prescribe 2D TOF at the pelvic area. Care must be taken to include the bifurcation of the femoral arteries (See figure 22.4)

(See figures 22.2, 22.3, 22.5, 22.6, 22.9 to 22.14)

Figure 22-1

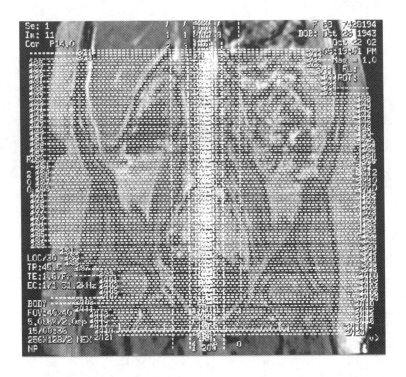

Figure 22-2

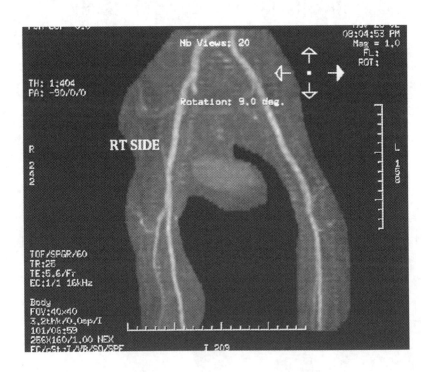

Figure 22-3

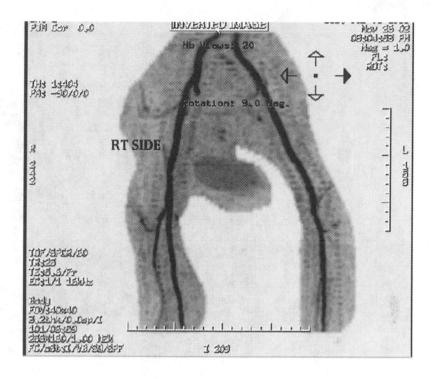

Figure 22-4

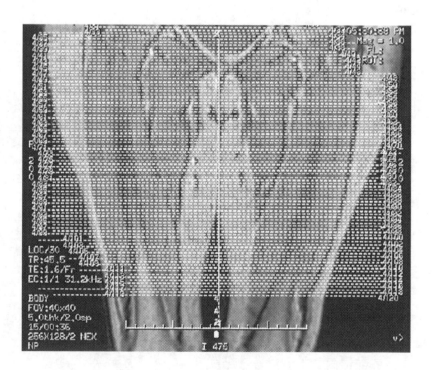

Figure 22-5

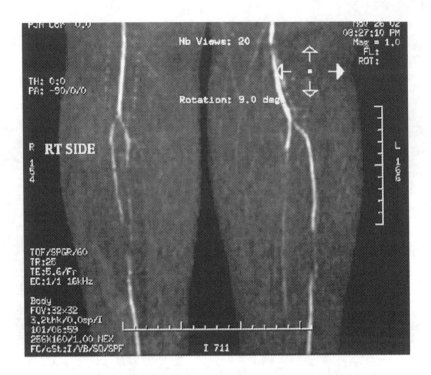

Figure 22-6

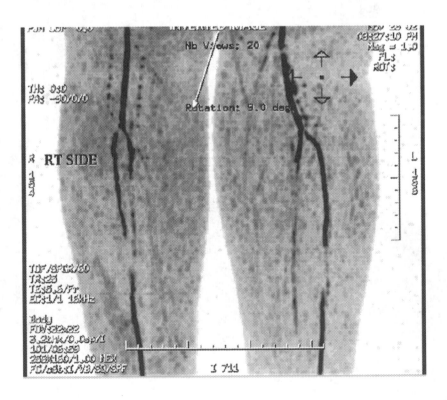

Figure 22-7

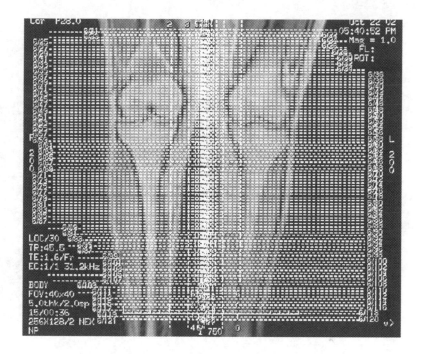

Figure 22-8

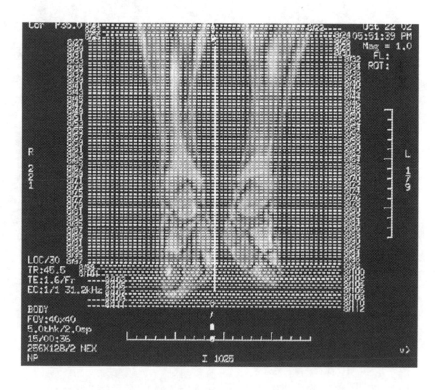

Figure 22-9

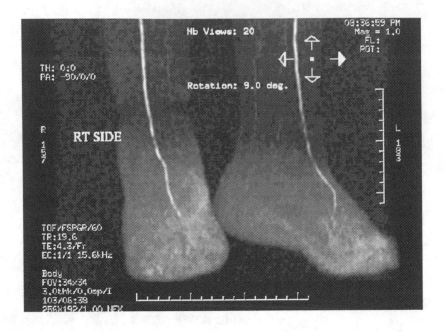

Figure 22-10

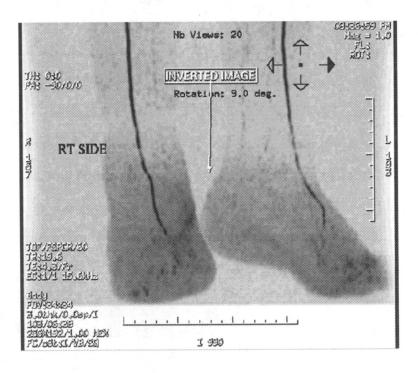

Figure 22-11

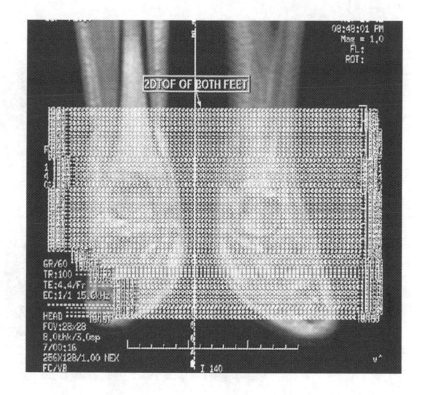

Figure 22-12

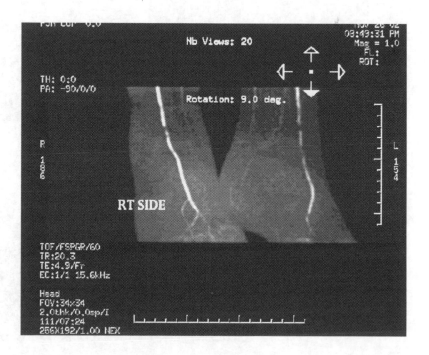

Figure 22-13

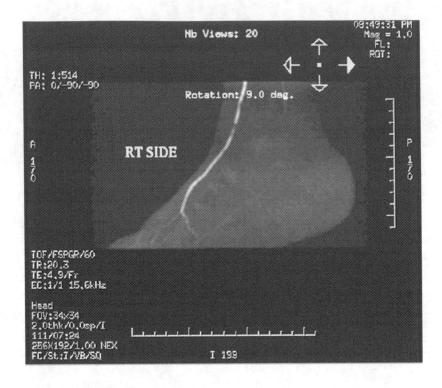

Figure 22-14

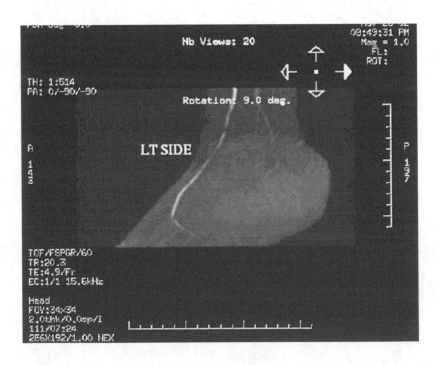

CHAPTER 23

SCANNING THE KNEE

SOME INDICATIONS TO SCAN A KNEE:

1. Wide range of knee disorders
2. Meniscal tears
3. Anterior and posterior cruciate ligament tears
4. Knee joint effusion
5. Baker's Cysts also known as Politeal cysts

COIL

The quadriture extremity coil is used

LAND MARKING

The longitudinal laser light is as close as possible to the center of the table. If the patient is too large then an offset can be set. For example, if examining the right knee, an offset can be measured and set accordingly. The horizontal laser light is crossing about ½ " below the apex of the patella.

POSITIONING

The patient is supine, feet first. The knee is positioned in the extremity quad knee coil. Foam pads are used to secure the knee tightly in place.

SUGGESTED PROTOCOL

1. A 3 plane FSE localizer is performed
2. Axial Pd Fat Sat
3. Sagittal Pd Fat Sat
4. Sagittal Pd no Fat Sat
5. Coronal Pd Fat Sat
6. Coronal Pd no Fat Sat
7. Sagittal T_1
8. If C+ T_1 Axial, T_1 Sagittal, T_1 Coronal all Fat Sat

Pd Coronal/Pd Coronal Fat Sat-

Pick an axial slice that demonstrates the intercondyloid fossa. The prescribed lines should be placed transversely and matching the end plates of the medial and lateral condyles (See figure 23.1 and 23.2).

SagiPd Fat Sat/Sagittal Pd no Fat Sat

Again, using the axial slice as explained in #1 above, but prescribing sagittal images, the lines are now placed parallel to the lateral aspect of the condyles (See figure 23.3).

T$_1$ Sagittal SE-

Prescribed the same as above (See figure 23.3).

PD FAT SAT axial-

Pick a sagittal image on which the patella is well demonstrated. The prescribed lines are placed transversely and slightly superior from the patella to the proximal portion of the tibia. Make sure that the image is ate the center of the field of view. As in all FAT SAT sequences, manual positioning must be performed (See figure 23.4).

HOW TO SCAN A KNEE

Figure 23-1   **AXIAL IMAGE SHOWING PD CORONAL PLANNING**

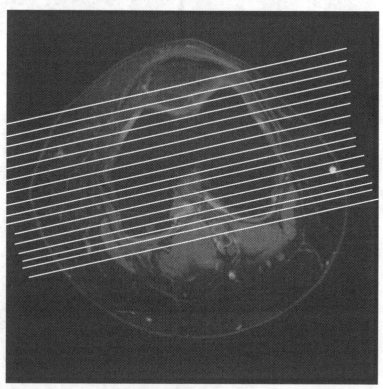

Figure 23-2

**AXIAL IMAGE SHOWING PD FAT SAT CORONAL
PLANNING**

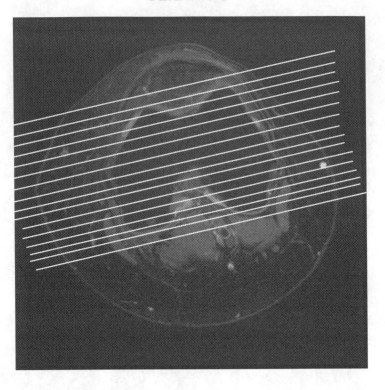

Figure 23-3

AXIAL IMAGE SHOWING SAGITTAL PLANNING

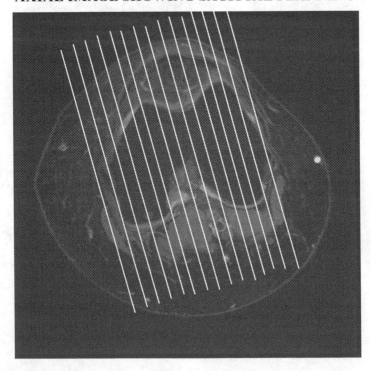

Figure 23-4

SAGITTAL IMAGE SHOWING AXIAL PLANNING

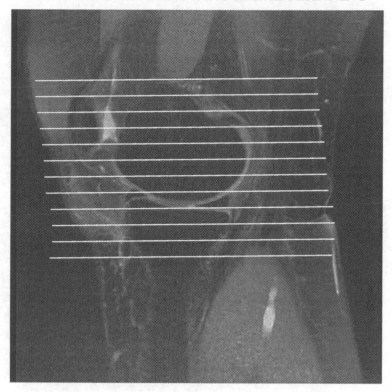

Figure 23-5

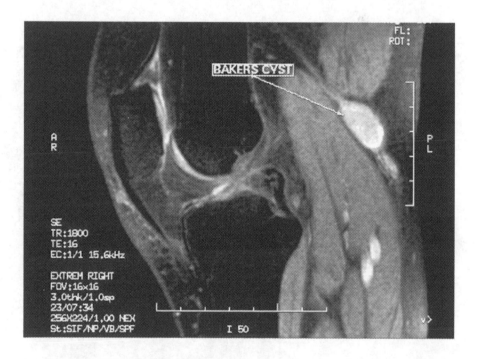

Figure 23-6   **SAGITTAL PD FAT SAT**

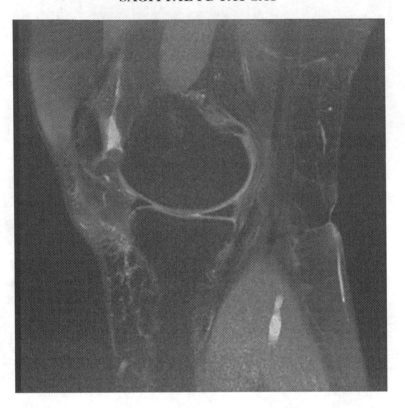

Figure 23-7

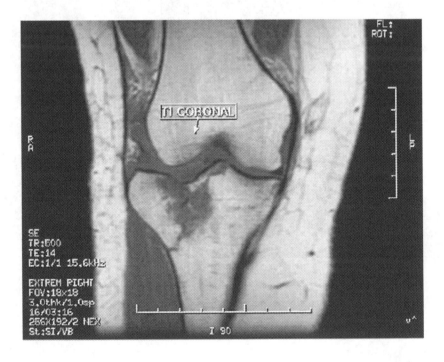

Figure 23-8

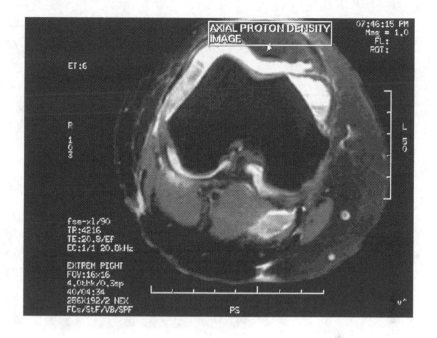

Figure 23-9

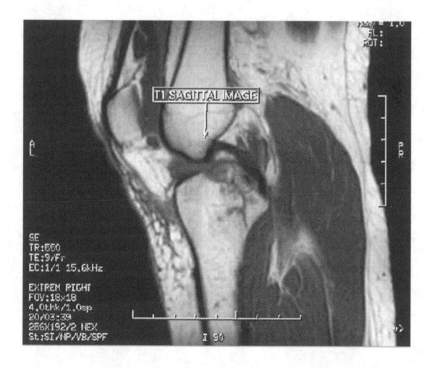

Figure 23-10

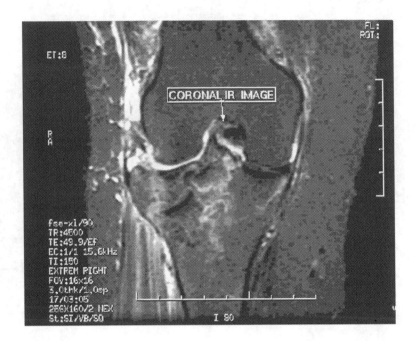

CHAPTER 24

SCANNING THE WRIST, THUMB, HAND

SOME INDICATIONS TO SCAN A WRIST, THUMB OR HAND:

1. Pain
2. Necrosis
3. Trauma
4. Carpal Tunnel syndrome
5. Ligament damage

COIL

The quad extremity coil can be used for this examination but the dedicated wrist coil is best. By using this coil, the fingers can also be imaged successfully. The hand must be very well secured with sponges and taped down. The elbow should also be supported with a sponge so as to relieve any pressure on the forearm.

LAND MARKING

The longitudinal laser light must run at the middle of the hand and the horizontal light is at the middle of the hand, if imaging the hand. If imaging the wrist, the horizontal light is at the carpal bones.

POSITIONING

The patient is prone and the hand is placed above the head in a small surface coil.

SUGGESTED PROTOCOL

1. A 3 plane FSE localizer is performed
2. Sagittal gradient
3. Axial T_2 FSE
4. Coronal FSE/IR
5. Coronal T_1 SE
6. Coronal gradient 3D

Axial T_2 FSE -

Select a mid coronal image to prescribe axial slices from top to bottom to cover the area of the carpal bones (see figure 24.1)

Coronals FSE/IR T_1 SE

Select a mid sagittal slice and prescribe from the anterior to the posterior aspect of the wrist (see figure 24.2).

Sagittal gradient -

Select a mid coronal image to prescribe the sagittal slices oriented from the left going to the right (see figure 24.3).

Coronal gradient 3D

Select a mid sagittal slice. As in all 3D sequences, this is a slab, or one thick slice. The slab is placed straight on the sagittal image.

(See figures 24.1 to 24.7)

Figure 24-1

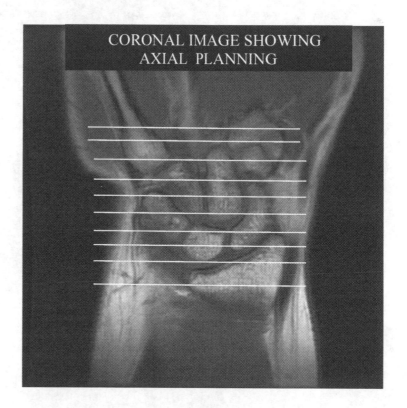

CORONAL IMAGE SHOWING
AXIAL PLANNING

Figure 24-2

Figure 24-3

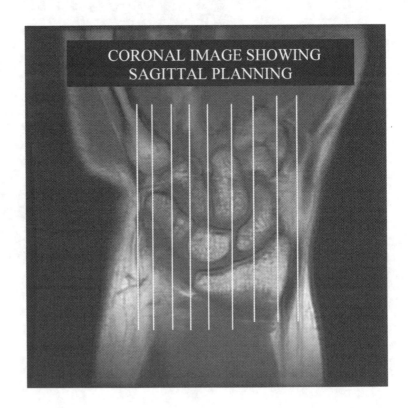

Figure 24-4

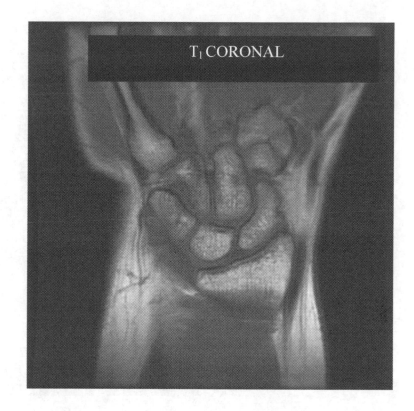

Figure 24-5

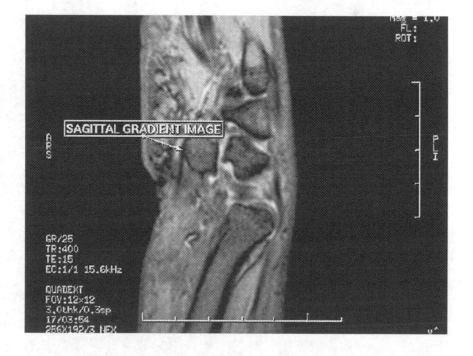

Figure 24-6

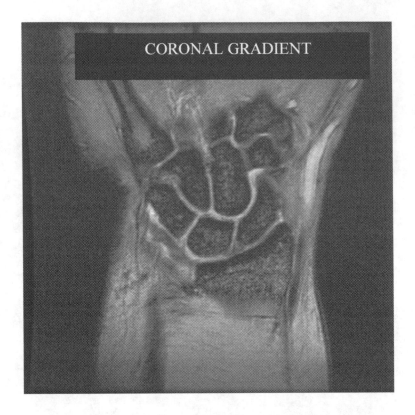

CORONAL GRADIENT

Figure 24-7

T$_1$ AXIAL IMAGE

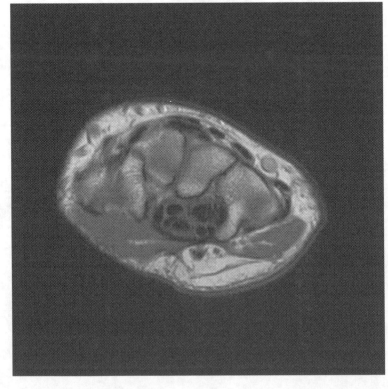

CHAPTER 25

SCANNING THE ANKLE

SOME INDICATIONS FOR SCANNING THE ANKLE

1. Soft tissue involvement
2. Tendon and ligament tears
3. Necrosis
4. Ankle joint evaluation
5. Osteomyelitis

COIL

The quad extremity coil is attached.

LAND MARKING

The longitudinal laser light is at the midline of the ankle. If the patient is too wide, then an offset is set in order to bring the ankle as close to the center as possible. The horizontal laser light is crossing the ankle joint.

POSITIONING

The patient is supine with the feet first. The feet are positioned in such a way that the toes are pointing upwards in the foot holder. Sponges and tape is used to secure the foot.

SUGGESTED PROTOCOL

A 3-plane localizer is performed utilizing:

1. A fast gradient pulse sequence
2. Sagittal T_1 FSE
3. Sagittal FSE, IR
4. Axial FSE T_2
5. Coronal FSE T_2
6. Coronal Stir

SAGITTALS

Select a mid coronal image. The prescribed lines are oriented from the left to the right to include the ankle joint at the center of the field of view. As for all the pulse sequences of this study, thin thickness and spacing must be used (3mm x .5 spacing) (See figure 25.1).

AXIAL T_2 FSE

Select a mid sagittal image demonstrating the calcaneous in full profile. The prescribed lines are placed from top to bottom to include the superior aspect of the ankle joint and the calcaneous. (See figure 25.2).

CORONALS

Select a mid sagittal image. The prescribed lines are placed from the left to the right. (See figure 24.3). In cases of suspected Osteomyelitis, pre FAT SAT images are performed and post T_1 axials, sagittals and coronals are performed.

(See figures 25.4 to 25.8)

Figure 25-1   **T_1 CORONAL IMAGE SHOWING SAGITTAL PLANNING**

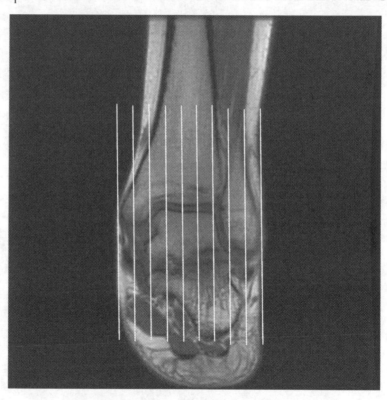

Figure 25-2   **T₁ SAGITTAL IMAGE SHOWING AXIAL PLANNING**

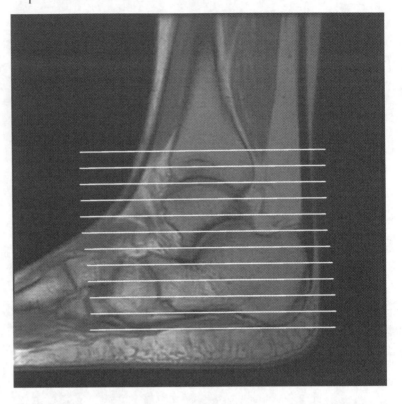

Figure 25-3   **T₁ SAGITTAL SHOWING CORONAL PLANNING**

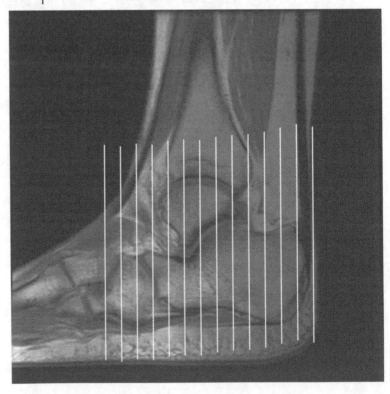

Figure 25-4   **SAGITTAL STIR**

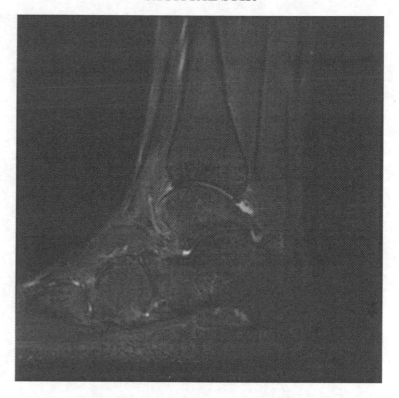

Figure 25-5   **T₁ CORONAL**

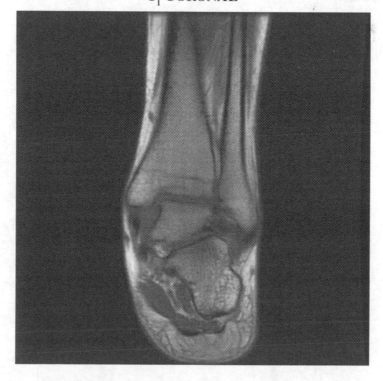

Figure 25-6   T₂ AXIAL ANKLE

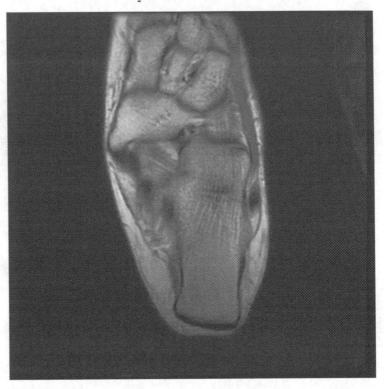

Figure 25-7   T₂ CORONAL

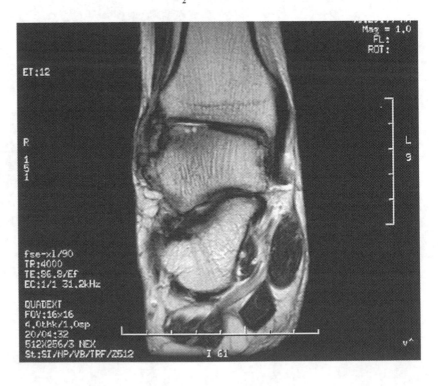

Figure 25-8   **AXIAL PD FAT SAT**

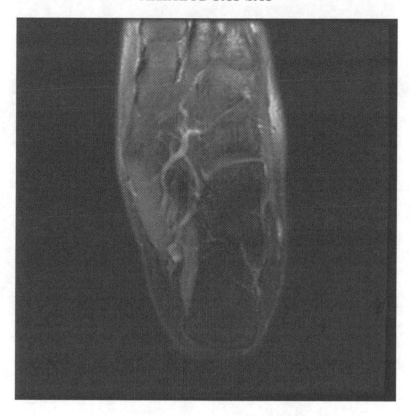

CHAPTER 26

SCANNING THE FOOT

SOME INDICATION FOR MRI OF THE FOOT

1. Trauma
2. Tumors
3. Infections

POSITIONING

The patient is supine with the feet first. The quad extremity coil is attached. The foot is positioned in such a way that the toes are pointing upwards and resting on the special opening in the coil. Foam pads and tape is used to secure the foot.

COIL

The dedicated extremity quad coil is used.

LAND MARKING

The longitudinal laser light is at the midline of the foot. The horizontal laser light is at the base of the phalanges.

SUGGESTED PROTOCOL

A 3-plane localizer is performed.

AXIALS

From the sagittal view prescribe axials. (See figure 26.2).

CORONALS

Use a sagittal image to prescribe coronal slices (See figure 26.3).

SAGITTALS

Pick an axial image that demonstrates the phalanges, and then prescribe the lines from left to right as in figure 26.4. In case of Osteomyelitis, pre FAT SAT images are done followed by gadolinium, then post T_1 pulse sequences in different planes.

Figure 26-1   **AXIAL FOOT SHOWING SAGITTAL PLANNING**

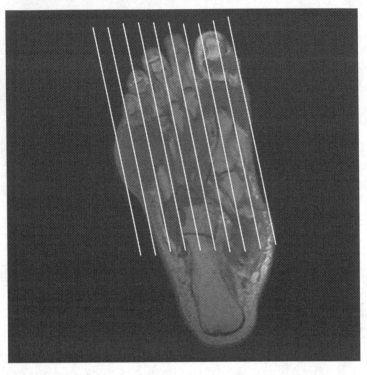

Figure 26-2   **SAGITTAL FOOT SHOWING AXIAL PLANNING**

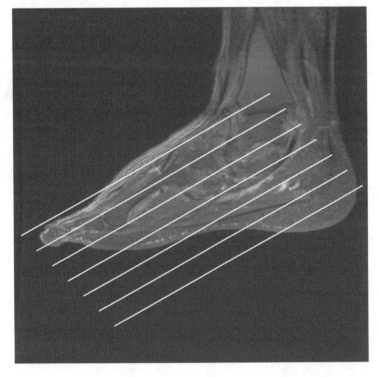

SAGITTAL IMAGE ILLUSTRATING
CORONAL PRESCRIPTION

Figure 26-3   **SAGITTAL IMAGE SHOWING CORONAL PLANNING**

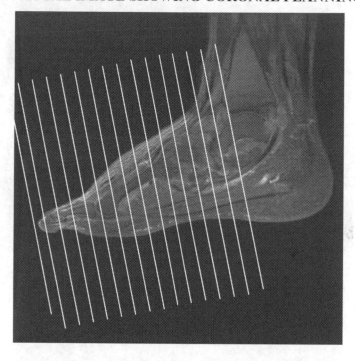

Figure 26-4   **AXIAL T₁ IMAGE**

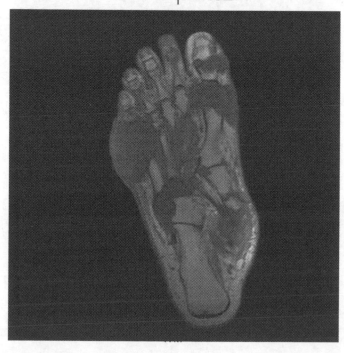

A result of figure 26-2

prescriptioning

213

Figure 26-5   **CORONAL PD FAT SAT**

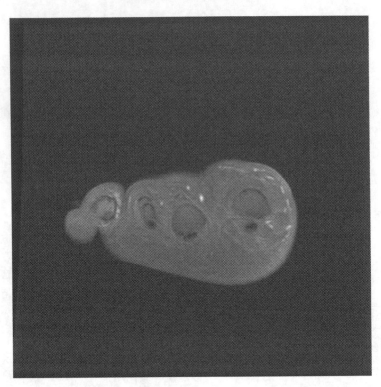

Printed in the United States
By Bookmasters